The Flavors of

BON APPÉTIT

2005

Grilled Corn on the Cob
with Jalapeño-Lime Butter (page 151)

The Flavors of
BON APPÉTIT
2005

from the Editors of Bon Appétit

Condé Nast Books

New York

For *Bon Appétit* Magazine

Barbara Fairchild, *Editor-in-Chief*
Tricia Callas O'Donnell, *Contributing Editor, Books*
Marcy MacDonald, *Editorial Operations Director*
Carri Marks Oosterbaan, *Editorial Production Director*
Michelle Danner, *Editorial Production Manager*
Sybil Shimazu Neubauer, *Editorial Administrator*
Marcia Hartmann Lewis, *Editorial Support*
Susan Champlin, *Text*
Shayna Sobol, *Copy Editor*
Gaylen Ducker Grody, *Research*
Elizabeth A. Matlin, *Index*

For Condé Nast Books

Lisa Faith Phillips, *Vice President and General Manager*
Tom Downing, *Direct Marketing Director*
Deborah Williams, *Operations Director*
Lyn Barris Hastings, *Senior Project Manager*
Fianna Reznik, *Direct Marketing Associate*
Elizabeth Walsh, *Inventory Manager*
Eric Killer, *Project Associate*

Design: Monica Elias and Ph.D

Front Jacket: Chocolate-Amaretti Tortes (page 204)
Facing Page: Top: Dilled Gravlax with Mustard Sauce (page 22)
            Middle: Wine-Braised Lamb Shanks with Herbes de Provence (page 65)
            Bottom: Lemon Crème Brûlée Tart (page 172)

Published by Condé Nast Books, Random House Direct, Inc., New York, New York.
A wholly owned subsidiary of Random House, Inc.

Printed in the United States of America

Library of Congress Cataloging-in-Publication Data is available upon request.

10 9 8 7 6 5 4 3 2 1

FIRST EDITION

Condé Nast Web Address: bonappetit.com
Bon Appétit Books Web Address: bonappetitbooks.com

Contents

Introduction

Imagine that someone handed you a round-the-world airline ticket and sent you off with just two instructions: Try a bite of every cuisine. And bring home your favorites.

That's your pleasurable assignment as you page through *The Flavors of Bon Appétit 2005.* You'll be on a journey that takes you from Southeast Asia to South America to the South of France and beyond, sampling the unique ingredients and flavors of each place, and bringing them into your home kitchen. The results are a dazzling marriage of the familiar and the exotic, new flavors transforming old favorites.

Needless to say, cooking in America has changed significantly since the days when using curry powder was considered daring, and the only fresh peppers around were red and green bells. We've moved into the world, culinarily speaking, and the world has come to us—into our grocery stores, farmers' markets, and specialty shops. These days, we're as likely to cook with hoisin sauce as with Worcestershire sauce, with Jamaican jerk seasoning as with seasoned salt.

Mojito-Marinated Chicken Breasts (page 75)

And here's something even more interesting: While we once would have scooped up a basketful of Asian spices in order to re-create an authentic Asian meal, or scoured the city for Indian ingredients so that we could prepare curry, dal, *raita,* and tandoori chicken (and while we certainly still do that), these ingredients have become familiar enough that we can now incorporate them into a wide variety of dishes—not just those for which they were originally intended. Thus the humble cheeseburger is jazzed up with the kick of poblano chiles (page 46). A steaming mug of hot chocolate gets a lift from Asian whole star anise (page 40). Chicken breasts take a Cuban twist with a rum-and-mint-flavored mojito marinade (page 75).

It is as if we have moved from coloring inside the lines to creating our very own masterpieces.

Black-Bottom Raspberry Cream Pie (page 181)

Of course, for those whose tastes reside stateside, there are plenty of beloved favorites here, too. Because this is *Bon Appétit,* the recipes are both straightforward and sophisticated, as simple to make as they are extraordinary to eat. Consider the Quick Apple Tart (page 173), for instance: With five ingredients and less than an hour's preparation time—baking included—you have a classic, all-American dessert that will wow your friends and family. And need we say more than "Black-Bottom Raspberry Cream Pie" (page 181)?

Clearly, when you're cooking with *Bon Appétit,* the options are wide open to you. You can be as daring or as traditional as you want. You can whip up a delicious after-work meal in no time flat, or spend all day Saturday preparing a dinner party for friends. You can use every spice in your pantry, or keep things perfectly simple (and simply perfect). Here's the secret: You can't go wrong.

The flavors of *Bon Appétit* are the flavors of the whole wide world. And they taste just like home.

Skewered Rosemary Shrimp
with Mint Pesto (page 20)

Starters

Appetizers

Soups

Beverages

Fried Calamari with Rouille, Cherry Peppers, and Lemon

QUICK ROUILLE

- 1 cup mayonnaise
- 1 tablespoon fresh lemon juice
- 2 teaspoons Hungarian sweet paprika
- 1 teaspoon cayenne pepper
- 1 large garlic clove, minced

CALAMARI

- ¼ cup olive oil
- 1 tablespoon dried crushed red pepper
- ½ cup chopped seeded pickled cherry peppers
- 1 teaspoon fresh lemon juice

  Vegetable oil (for frying)

- 1 cup yellow cornmeal
- 1 cup all purpose flour
- 2 teaspoons salt
- 1 teaspoon ground black pepper
- 2 pounds fresh or thawed frozen small calamari, bodies cleaned and cut into ½-inch-wide rings, tentacles reserved

- 2 lemons, each cut into 6 wedges

FOR QUICK ROUILLE: Stir all ingredients in small bowl to blend. Season to taste with salt and pepper. (*Can be made 1 day ahead. Cover and refrigerate.*)

FOR CALAMARI: Heat olive oil in heavy large skillet over medium-high heat. Add crushed red pepper; stir 30 seconds. Add cherry peppers (mixture may splatter); stir 30 seconds. Remove from heat. Stir in 1 teaspoon lemon juice. Season with salt and pepper.

Add enough vegetable oil to another large skillet to come 1 inch up sides of pan. Heat vegetable oil to 375°F.

Whisk cornmeal, flour, salt, and pepper in medium bowl to blend. Toss calamari rings and tentacles in flour mixture, shaking off excess. Working in batches, fry calamari in oil until brown and crisp, about 3 minutes. Using slotted spoon, transfer calamari to paper towels to drain. Sprinkle with salt. Transfer to large bowl.

Rewarm cherry pepper mixture. Drizzle over calamari; toss to coat. Serve with rouille and lemon wedges.

6 TO 8 SERVINGS

Grilled Chile Salsa with Rice Crackers

- 6 large garlic cloves, unpeeled
- 4 large plum tomatoes (¾ to 1 pound total)
- 4 3-inch-long serrano chiles
- 4 large shallots, peeled, halved through root end
- 2 tablespoons vegetable oil

- 1 cup chopped fresh cilantro
- 8 teaspoons fresh lime juice

    Purchased rice crackers

Prepare barbecue (medium-high heat). Combine garlic, tomatoes, chiles, and shallots in medium bowl. Add oil and toss to coat. Arrange vegetables on barbecue; sprinkle with salt and pepper. Grill until charred, turning occasionally, about 8 minutes. Using tongs, transfer garlic and vegetables to plate and cool.

Peel garlic; chop coarsely. Chop tomatoes. Cut chiles in half lengthwise; discard seeds and chop chiles coarsely. Chop shallots. Combine all vegetables in medium bowl. Add cilantro and lime juice. Blend well; season with salt and pepper. *(Salsa can be made 8 hours ahead. Cover and chill. Bring to room temperature and stir before using.)*

Transfer salsa to serving bowl. Serve with rice crackers.

MAKES ABOUT 2 CUPS

Lobster Macaroni and Cheese

1	1¾- to 2-pound live lobster
2	tablespoons olive oil, divided
12	large shrimp, peeled, deveined, shells reserved
1	cup chopped onion
¾	cup chopped peeled carrots
¾	cup chopped celery
2	garlic cloves, peeled, flattened
1	Turkish bay leaf
1	tablespoon tomato paste
¼	cup Cognac or brandy
3	cups water
4	tablespoons (½ stick) butter, divided
2	tablespoons all purpose flour
1	cup whipping cream
1½	cups grated Fontina cheese (about 6 ounces)
8	ounces shell or gemelli pasta
6	ounces fresh crabmeat, picked over
2	tablespoons chopped fresh chives

Plunge lobster headfirst into pot of boiling water; boil 4 minutes. Using tongs, transfer to cutting board. Cut off tail and claws. Crack tail and claws and remove meat. Cut meat into 1/2-inch pieces. Cut body and shells into 2-inch pieces. Chill meat; reserve shells.

Heat 1 tablespoon oil in heavy large skillet over medium-high heat. Add lobster body, lobster shells, and shrimp shells to skillet and sauté 4 minutes. Add onion and next 4 ingredients; sauté 6 minutes. Add tomato paste; stir 1 minute. Remove from heat; stir in Cognac. Add 3 cups water; bring to boil. Reduce heat, cover, and simmer 30 minutes.

Strain mixture into bowl, pressing on solids to extract liquid; discard solids. Set stock aside. Heat 1 tablespoon oil in same skillet over medium-high heat. Add shrimp; sauté until just opaque in center, about 3 minutes. Cool slightly. Coarsely chop shrimp.

Melt 2 tablespoons butter in large saucepan over medium heat. Add flour; stir 1 minute. Add stock and cream; simmer until sauce is reduced to 2 cups, about 5 minutes. Add cheese; stir until smooth. Season with salt and pepper. Remove from heat.

Meanwhile, cook pasta in large pot of boiling salted water until just tender but still firm to bite. Drain. Stir lobster, shrimp, pasta, crab, and 2 tablespoons butter into sauce. Stir over medium-low heat until heated through, about 2 minutes. Season with salt and pepper. Serve topped with chives.

6 SERVINGS

Prosciutto-Wrapped Figs with Gorgonzola and Walnuts

9	large fresh black Mission figs, stemmed, halved
18	1x5-inch thin strips prosciutto (about 3 ounces)
3	tablespoons Gorgonzola cheese
18	large walnut pieces, toasted

Preheat broiler. Cover large rimmed baking sheet with foil. Wrap each fig half with 1 prosciutto strip; place on prepared sheet. Broil until prosciutto chars slightly on edges, about 1 1/2 minutes. Turn figs; broil about 1 1/2 minutes longer, watching closely to prevent burning. Place 1/2 teaspoon Gorgonzola atop each fig half. Top each with walnut piece. Serve warm or at room temperature.

MAKES 18

If fresh figs aren't available, dried black Mission figs can be substituted here; look for ones that are soft and moist.

Sliced Radishes and Watercress on Buttered Ficelle

¼ cup unsalted butter, room temperature
18 thin diagonal slices ficelle or other narrow baguette
  Fleur de sel (fine French sea salt)
1 small bunch watercress, trimmed
4 watermelon radishes or other large radishes, very thinly sliced
  Edible flowers or daikon radish sprouts* (optional)

Spread some butter over bread slices. Sprinkle with fleur de sel. Top each bread slice with 2 watercress sprigs. Spread 1 side of each radish slice with butter. Place 2 radish slices atop watercress, buttered side down, overlapping slightly if necessary to fit. Top with flowers or sprouts, if desired. *(Can be prepared 1 hour ahead. Cover and let stand at room temperature.)*

*Available at some supermarkets, farmers' markets, and specialty foods stores.

MAKES 18

Ficelle, a slender demi-baguette available mostly from artisanal bakeries, makes elegant slices, but any narrow French baguette will work. Team this dish with the recipe below and flutes of brut Champagne.

Bresaola with Arugula, Fennel, and Manchego Cheese

3 tablespoons olive oil
1 tablespoon fresh lemon juice
1 4-ounce package sliced bresaola*
54 (about) arugula leaves
1 medium fennel bulb, halved lengthwise, thinly sliced crosswise
1 4-ounce piece Manchego or Parmesan cheese, shaved into strips

Whisk olive oil and lemon juice in small bowl to blend; set dressing aside. Place 1 bresaola slice on work surface with 1 long side parallel to edge. Place 3 arugula leaves at 1 short end so that leaves extend past 1 long side. Top with layer of sliced fennel, then 2 cheese strips. Sprinkle with pepper. Drizzle with ½ teaspoon dressing. Starting at filled end, roll up bresaola, enclosing filling. Arrange, seam side down, on platter. Repeat with remaining ingredients to form 18 rolls total. *(Can be made 4 hours ahead. Cover with plastic wrap; chill. Before serving, let stand 30 minutes at room temperature.)*

*Available at Italian markets and some specialty foods stores.

MAKES 18

Prosciutto is more familiar in this type of appetizer, but bresaola, beef fillet cured in a similar fashion, gives it a fresh interpretation. When paired with golden Spanish Manchego, the combination is deliciously bold in flavor.

Fresh Crab Dip

    1 8-ounce package cream cheese, room temperature
    3 tablespoons mayonnaise
    3 tablespoons fresh lemon juice
    2 tablespoons finely chopped red onion
    1 tablespoon prepared white horseradish
    1 teaspoon (or more) Worcestershire sauce
   ¼ teaspoon hot pepper sauce
    8 ounces fresh crabmeat, picked over

       Chopped fresh parsley
       Toasted baguette slices and crackers
       Assorted crudités (such as carrot, celery, and jicama sticks; bell pepper strips; and halved
          radishes)

Combine first 5 ingredients in medium bowl. Add 1 teaspoon Worcestershire sauce and hot pepper sauce; blend well. Mix in crabmeat. Season dip to taste with salt, pepper, and additional Worcestershire sauce, if desired. *(Can be made 1 day ahead. Cover; chill. Let stand 2 hours at room temperature before serving.)*

Place dip on platter. Sprinkle with parsley. Surround with toasts, crackers, and crudités.

MAKES ABOUT 3 CUPS

Sweet and Spicy Herbed Hazelnuts

       Vegetable oil
    4 cups hazelnuts, toasted, husked
    1 cup (packed) dark brown sugar
   ⅓ cup coarsely chopped fresh rosemary
    1 tablespoon coarse kosher salt
    5 dashes of hot pepper sauce

Preheat oven to 350°F. Brush 13x9x2-inch baking pan and large rimmed baking sheet generously with oil. Mix hazelnuts, brown sugar, rosemary, salt, and hot pepper sauce in large bowl to blend. Transfer to prepared baking pan. Bake until sugar melts and coats nuts, stirring every 5 minutes, about 20 minutes. Transfer to prepared baking sheet. Cool completely. Break hazelnuts apart and store in airtight container at room temperature. *(Can be made 5 days ahead.)*

MAKES 4 CUPS

Citrus-Marinated Olives

  3 cups extra-virgin olive oil
  1 large orange
  4 sprigs fresh rosemary
  2 dried ancho chiles,* torn in half, stemmed, seeded
  1 lemon, quartered
  1 teaspoon whole black peppercorns
1¾ pounds Kalamata olives with pits

The marinade for these olives is aromatic with citrus, rosemary, and ancho chiles. The longer these olives marinate (up to a week), the better they'll taste.

Place 3 cups extra-virgin olive oil in heavy large saucepan. Using vegetable peeler, remove peel from orange in strips. Add orange peel to saucepan. Add rosemary sprigs, ancho chiles, lemon quarters, and whole peppercorns. Heat olive oil mixture over medium heat just until warm, about 3 minutes. Place olives in medium bowl. Pour oil mixture over. Let marinate at room temperature 1 day. *(Can be made 1 week ahead. Cover; chill.)*

Ancho chiles are available at some supermarkets, Latin American markets, and specialty foods stores.

20 SERVINGS

Papaya Spring Rolls with Peanut Sauce

½ cup chunky peanut butter
⅓ cup water
2 tablespoons unseasoned rice vinegar
2 tablespoons fish sauce (such as nam pla or nuoc nam)*
2 teaspoons hot chili paste (such as sambal oelek)*

24 6-inch-diameter rice paper rounds**
24 large fresh basil leaves
48 large fresh mint leaves
1½ large firm but ripe papayas, halved lengthwise then crosswise, seeded, peeled, cut
      crosswise into ½-inch-thick strips
1 unpeeled English hothouse cucumber, cut into ¼-inch-thick 2½-inch-long strips
48 small fresh cilantro sprigs

Whisk first 5 ingredients in bowl. (*Peanut sauce can be made 3 days ahead. Cover and chill. Rewhisk before serving.*)

Fill large bowl with warm water. Working in batches, soak 3 rice paper rounds in water until softened, about 2 minutes. Remove rounds from water and arrange in single layer on work surface. Place 1 basil leaf in center of each round. Place 2 mint leaves atop each basil leaf. Place 2 papaya strips, then 2 cucumber strips atop mint. Arrange 2 cilantro sprigs atop cucumber. Fold 1 edge of each round over filling. Fold in ends. Roll up rice paper rounds tightly, enclosing filling. Transfer to platter. Repeat with remaining rice paper rounds. Cover with moist paper towel, then plastic wrap; chill. *(Can be made 8 hours ahead. Keep chilled.)* Serve rolls with peanut sauce.

Fish sauce is available in the Asian foods section of many supermarkets and at Asian markets.
**Thin Thai or Vietnamese wrappers are made from rice flour and known as banh trang. Available in the Asian foods section of many supermarkets and at Asian markets nationwide.

MAKES 24

Baked Feta with Onion and Olives

- ⅓ cup balsamic vinegar
- 3 tablespoons extra-virgin olive oil
- 1 teaspoon caraway seeds, toasted

  Nonstick vegetable oil spray
- 2 8-ounce packages feta cheese, cut horizontally in half to make four ½-inch-thick squares
- ⅓ cup very thinly sliced red onion
- ⅓ cup pitted Kalamata olives, quartered lengthwise
  Crusty French bread slices
  Fresh dill sprigs

Preheat oven to 450°F. Blend vinegar, olive oil, and toasted caraway seeds in blender. Season vinaigrette to taste with salt and pepper.

Coat nonstick rimmed baking sheet with nonstick spray. Place cheese on prepared baking sheet. Bake until heated through, about 5 minutes. Remove cheese from oven. Preheat broiler. Broil cheese until crusty and golden brown, about 5 minutes.

Spoon vinaigrette onto platter; place cheese atop vinaigrette. Sprinkle with onion and olives. Surround with bread slices; garnish with dill and serve.

6 TO 8 SERVINGS

Mediterranean Dinner for 8

Baked Feta with Onion and Olives
(at left)

Grilled Leg of Lamb with Mustard and Rosemary
(page 58)

Green Bean and Radicchio Salad with Roasted Beets and Balsamic Red Onions
(halve recipe; page 155)

Roasted Potatoes

Pinot Noir

Strawberries in Red Wine Syrup with Crème Fraîche
(page 192)

Skewered Rosemary Shrimp with Mint Pesto

MINT PESTO

½ cup pine nuts, toasted

3 garlic cloves, peeled

2 tablespoons (packed) feta cheese

2 tablespoons (packed) Parmesan cheese

1 tablespoon coarsely chopped jalapeño chile

½ teaspoon salt

½ teaspoon ground black pepper

2 cups (packed) fresh mint leaves

2 tablespoons fresh lemon juice

⅓ cup extra-virgin olive oil

SHRIMP

24 large uncooked shrimp (about 2 pounds), peeled, deveined, tails left intact

2 tablespoons olive oil

2 garlic cloves, minced

1 tablespoon chopped fresh parsley

3 tablespoons fresh lemon juice

24 4-inch-long woody rosemary sprigs

FOR MINT PESTO: Combine first 7 ingredients in processor. Using on/off turns, process until mixture is smooth. Add mint leaves and lemon juice; process until smooth, stopping occasionally to scrape down sides of bowl. Gradually add oil and process until mint pesto is smooth and creamy. (*Can be made 1 day ahead; cover and refrigerate.*)

FOR SHRIMP: Preheat broiler. Sprinkle shrimp with salt and pepper. Whisk oil, garlic, and parsley in medium bowl to blend. Add shrimp; toss to coat. Let stand at room temperature 15 minutes. Arrange shrimp in single layer on broiler pan. Broil until opaque in center, about 2 minutes per side. Transfer to large bowl; sprinkle with lemon juice and toss with ½ cup mint pesto. Starting at base end of rosemary sprigs, skewer 1 shrimp on each sprig. Arrange on platter and serve.

MAKES 24

Smoked Trout Mousse with Soy Chips

6 ounces boneless smoked trout fillets (one and a half 4.5-ounce packages), coarsely broken
¾ cup crème fraîche* (about 6 ounces)
1½ tablespoons minced shallot
1½ teaspoons fresh lemon juice
¾ teaspoon finely grated lemon peel

48 soy chips or thick-cut potato chips
Finely chopped fresh chives

Place fish in processor. Using on/off turns, finely chop fish. Transfer to bowl. Add crème fraîche, shallot, lemon juice, and lemon peel; stir gently to blend. Season mousse with salt and pepper. (*Can be made 1 day ahead. Cover and chill.*)

Arrange chips on platter. Spoon mousse into pastry bag fitted with ½-inch plain round tip. Pipe mousse onto each chip; sprinkle with chopped fresh chives and serve.

Available at many supermarkets nationwide.

8 SERVINGS

Dilled Gravlax with Mustard Sauce

GRAVLAX

- 1 teaspoon whole white peppercorns
- 1 teaspoon whole black peppercorns
- 1 teaspoon coriander seeds
- 2 tablespoons sea salt
- 2 teaspoons sugar

- 1 1-pound salmon fillet, skin on
- 1 cup chopped fresh dill, divided

SAUCE

- 2 tablespoons honey mustard
- 1 tablespoon distilled white vinegar
- 3 tablespoons grapeseed oil or canola oil
- 2 tablespoons chopped fresh dill
- ¼ teaspoon salt

  Mini pumpernickel or brioche toasts
  Dill sprigs

FOR GRAVLAX: Heat all peppercorns and coriander seeds in small skillet over medium-high heat until spices are fragrant and seeds jump slightly, shaking skillet frequently, about 2 minutes. Crush spices in mortar with pestle or transfer to work surface, cover with kitchen towel (not terry cloth), and crush with mallet or bottom of heavy pan. Transfer spices to small bowl. Mix in salt and sugar.

Using small sharp knife, poke 12 small holes through skin of salmon. Rub ⅓ of spice mixture over skin. Sprinkle ⅓ cup chopped dill in bottom of 7x7x2-inch or 8x8x2-inch glass baking dish. Place salmon, skin side down, atop dill. Rub remaining spice mixture into top of salmon. Press ⅔ cup chopped dill onto salmon. Cover with plastic wrap, pressing directly onto fish. Place plate or another pan atop plastic. Place heavy cans on plate. Refrigerate 2 to 3 days.

FOR SAUCE: Whisk honey mustard and white vinegar in small bowl to blend. Gradually whisk in oil. Stir in chopped fresh dill and salt. Season with ground black pepper. (*Sauce can be made 3 days ahead. Cover and refrigerate.*)

Scrape spices and dill off both sides of salmon (some spice mixture will remain). Using knife with long thin blade, thinly slice salmon diagonally at 45-degree angle from top of fillet toward skin.

Arrange toasts on platter; top with salmon slices, sauce, and dill sprigs.

4 SERVINGS

Ricotta- and Walnut-Stuffed Artichokes

⅓ cup fresh lemon juice
6 large artichokes

1 cup plus 2 tablespoons walnuts, toasted
1 16-ounce container whole-milk ricotta cheese
½ cup extra-virgin olive oil, divided
1 garlic clove, chopped
1 teaspoon salt
¼ teaspoon ground white pepper
¼ teaspoon ground nutmeg
¼ cup coarsely chopped fresh Italian parsley

¾ cup water
½ cup dry white wine

Fill large bowl with cold water; add lemon juice. Cut off stem and top 2 inches from 1 artichoke. Using scissors, cut off pointy ends of outer artichoke leaves. Using melon baller, scoop out fuzzy choke from center of artichoke, forming opening. Place artichoke in lemon water. Repeat with remaining artichokes. Bring large pot of salted water to boil. Add artichokes and cook until artichoke hearts are tender when pierced with metal skewer, about 15 minutes. Drain. Cool to room temperature.

Coarsely chop walnuts in processor. Transfer 2 tablespoons chopped walnuts to small bowl and reserve. Add ricotta cheese, ¼ cup olive oil, garlic, salt, white pepper, and nutmeg to walnuts in processor; process until well blended. Transfer ricotta mixture to bowl. Stir in parsley. Season to taste with additional salt and white pepper. Using teaspoon and fingertips as aids, spoon ricotta mixture into center of each artichoke, then spoon some mixture between artichoke leaves. Pour remaining ¼ cup olive oil into 13x9x2-inch glass or ceramic baking dish. Arrange stuffed artichokes in dish. (*Artichokes can be prepared 6 hours ahead. Cover and refrigerate.*)

Preheat oven to 375°F. Pour ¾ cup water and white wine into bottom of dish with artichokes. Cover dish with aluminum foil and bake until artichokes are very tender and stuffing is slightly firm, about 40 minutes. Uncover and sprinkle reserved 2 tablespoons chopped walnuts over artichokes. Bake uncovered 10 minutes longer. Let stand 10 minutes and serve.

6 SERVINGS

This dish is inspired by the marriage of ricotta and walnuts that makes Ligurian *pansotti* (triangular "pot-bellied" ravioli) with walnut sauce a timeless favorite. Serve the artichokes as a plated first course or quarter them and offer as part of an antipasto platter along with prosciutto, roasted red peppers, and marinated olives and mushrooms.

Fava Bean Crostini with Pecorino and Lemon Oil

1½	cups shelled fava beans (about 1½ pounds in pods) or thawed frozen baby lima beans
8	tablespoons extra-virgin olive oil, divided
10	garlic cloves, flattened
1	cup water
24	⅓-inch-thick diagonal slices French-bread baguette
¾	cup grated Pecorino Romano cheese
	Lemon-infused olive oil* (optional)

Fresh fava beans are often available in the spring at farmers' markets and Italian and Middle Eastern markets. If you can't find them, substitute frozen lima beans.

If using fava beans, boil in large pot of water 3 minutes. Drain. Transfer to large bowl of ice water. Drain again and peel.

Meanwhile, heat 6 tablespoons olive oil in heavy large saucepan over low heat. Add garlic. Cover and cook until garlic is very tender and beginning to dissolve into oil (do not allow garlic to brown), stirring occasionally, about 30 minutes. Add fava beans or thawed lima beans and 1 cup water. Cook over medium heat until beans begin to break apart, stirring often, about 20 minutes. Mash until mixture resembles coarse puree. Season to taste with salt and pepper.

Preheat oven to 350°F. Arrange bread slices on large baking sheet. Brush with remaining 2 tablespoons olive oil. Bake until golden brown, about 15 minutes. Cool completely. (*Can be made 1 day ahead. Cover and chill bean mixture. Store toasts airtight at room temperature.*)

Preheat broiler. Spread bean mixture onto toasts. Sprinkle with cheese. Broil until golden, about 2 minutes. Drizzle with lemon oil, if desired. Transfer to platter and serve.

*Available at some supermarkets and specialty foods stores.

MAKES 24

Tomato Gazpacho with Tower of Crab

SOUP

- 2 pounds plum tomatoes (about 12 large), cored, quartered
- 1 1-pound English hothouse cucumber, peeled, cubed
- 1 large red bell pepper, quartered, seeded
- 1 large yellow bell pepper, quartered, seeded
- ½ 8-ounce white onion, diced
- 2 large garlic cloves, peeled
- ¼ cup olive oil
- ¼ cup white wine vinegar
- ⅛ teaspoon cayenne pepper

CRAB SALAD

- ¼ cup chopped shallots
- ¼ cup mayonnaise
- 2 tablespoons minced fresh chives
- 1½ tablespoons fresh lemon juice
- 1 tablespoon ketchup
- ⅛ teaspoon cayenne pepper
- 1 pound lump crabmeat, picked over, broken into small lumps

  Purchased croutons
  Finely diced peeled English hothouse cucumber
  Finely diced red and yellow bell peppers
  Chopped fresh chives

FOR SOUP: Working in batches, puree first 8 ingredients in blender. Strain puree through sieve into large bowl, pressing hard on solids to extract as much pulp and liquid as possible. Whisk cayenne pepper into soup; season to taste with salt. Cover; refrigerate until cold, at least 3 hours. *(Can be made 1 day ahead. Keep refrigerated.)*

FOR CRAB SALAD: Combine first 6 ingredients in medium bowl; whisk to blend. Fold in crabmeat. Season with salt. Line 8 small deep glasses or custard cups with plastic wrap, leaving overhang. Divide salad equally among prepared cups (about ⅓ cup for each). Press salad to compact and conform to shape of container. Cover with overhang. Chill until cold, at least 1 hour and up to 8 hours.

Open plastic on top of salads. Turn out each salad into shallow soup bowl. Peel off plastic. Carefully pour soup into each bowl around crab salad. Sprinkle soup with croutons, finely diced cucumber, bell peppers, and chopped chives.

8 SERVINGS

Chilled Avocado and Mint Soup

    4   cups diced peeled avocados (about 4 medium)
    3¼ cups chilled buttermilk
    5   tablespoons fresh lime juice
    ¼   cup chopped green onions
    ¼   cup chopped fresh cilantro
    1   teaspoon minced seeded serrano chile
    1   teaspoon chili powder
    6   tablespoons chopped fresh mint leaves, divided
    3   cups (or more) low-salt chicken broth

    1   cup diced seeded tomatoes

Combine first 7 ingredients in processor. Add 4 tablespoons mint; blend until smooth. Transfer to large bowl. Gradually whisk in 3 cups broth. Season soup to taste with salt and pepper. Cover; chill until cold, about 2 hours. (*Can be made 6 hours ahead. Keep chilled. Thin with more broth by ¼ cupfuls, if desired. Rewhisk before serving.*)

Ladle soup into bowls. Garnish with diced tomatoes and remaining 2 tablespoons mint.

8 SERVINGS

Miso Soup with Shrimp and Watercress

3 14½-ounce cans low-salt chicken broth
¼ cup soy sauce
2 tablespoons mirin (sweet Japanese rice wine)
1 tablespoon minced peeled fresh ginger
1½ cups shredded carrots (about 3½ ounces)

5 tablespoons yellow miso (fermented soybean paste)

1½ pounds uncooked peeled deveined small shrimp
2 cups watercress, thick stems removed
¾ cup thinly sliced green onions
¾ teaspoon hot chili oil

Mirin, miso paste, and hot chili oil are all available in the Asian foods section of some supermarkets and at Asian markets.

Bring first 4 ingredients to boil in heavy medium saucepan over medium-high heat. Add carrots. Reduce heat to low; cover and simmer until carrots are crisp-tender, about 3 minutes.

Place miso in medium bowl. Whisk in ½ cup hot broth mixture. Return miso-broth mixture to same saucepan. (*Can be made 2 hours ahead. Cover and let stand at room temperature.*)

Bring soup to boil. Turn off heat. Mix in shrimp, watercress, and green onions. Cover and let stand until shrimp are cooked through, about 4 minutes. Stir in chili oil; divide soup equally among 4 bowls.

4 SERVINGS

Egg Ribbon and Parmesan Soup

3 large eggs
¾ cup grated Parmesan cheese, divided
6 cups low-salt chicken broth
¾ cup tiny pasta (such as acini di pepe or orzo)
  Chopped fresh Italian parsley

Whisk eggs and 3 tablespoons Parmesan cheese in small bowl to blend. Bring chicken broth to simmer in large pot. Add pasta. Cover and simmer until pasta is tender, about 6 minutes. Gradually add egg mixture to soup, stirring constantly until egg ribbons form, about 1 minute. Simmer 1 minute longer. Ladle soup into bowls. Sprinkle with parsley. Serve, passing remaining cheese separately.

4 SERVINGS

Scallop Tea Rice

1½ cups short-grain rice (such as sushi rice)
2½ cups bottled clam juice, divided
 3 tablespoons soy sauce, divided
 3 tablespoons sake, divided
 2 teaspoons minced peeled fresh ginger
 1 teaspoon sugar
 ½ teaspoon coarse kosher salt

 2 tablespoons loose green tea leaves or tea leaves from about 6 tea bags
 2 cups boiling water

 8 ounces sea scallops (about 12), side muscles removed

 1 4-ounce jar salmon roe (caviar)
 2 teaspoons white sesame seeds, toasted
 1 green onion, thinly sliced
 Wasabi paste*

Rinse rice in strainer under cold running water until water runs clear; drain well. Transfer rice to heavy medium saucepan. Add 2 cups clam juice, 1 tablespoon soy sauce, 1 tablespoon sake, ginger, sugar, and salt; bring to boil. Reduce heat to medium-low, cover, and simmer 10 minutes. Remove from heat; let stand, covered, until all liquid is absorbed and rice is tender, about 10 minutes.

Place green tea leaves in medium teapot. Pour 2 cups boiling water over; cover and let steep while preparing scallops.

Bring remaining 1/2 cup clam juice, 2 tablespoons soy sauce, and 2 tablespoons sake to boil in small skillet. Add scallops; cover and reduce heat to medium-low. Cook 30 seconds. Turn scallops over; cover and cook 30 seconds. Using slotted spoon, transfer scallops to plate; reserve cooking liquid in skillet. Slice each scallop in half horizontally to create 2 rounds.

Divide rice among 4 shallow soup bowls. Spoon reserved scallop cooking liquid around rice. Arrange scallops, cut side up, atop rice. Sprinkle salmon roe, sesame seeds, and green onion over. Strain hot tea over scallops. Serve, passing wasabi alongside.

Available in tubes in the Asian foods section of some supermarkets and at Japanese markets.

4 SERVINGS

Brewed green tea is a delicious, aromatic broth for scallops in this refined rendition of Japan's *ochazuke*, or "tea rice." The comforting soup-like dish evolved from using hot tea to rinse out rice bowls at the end of meals. Serve this as a first course, followed by teriyaki-marinated chicken or salmon and some steamed Asian greens.

Parsnip and Apple Soup

    3 Granny Smith apples (about 1½ pounds), divided
    1 tablespoon olive oil
    5 large shallots, sliced
 1¼ pounds medium parsnips, peeled, cut into ½-inch-thick rounds
 1¼ teaspoons ground coriander
    5 cups (or more) low-salt chicken broth

       Plain nonfat yogurt, stirred to loosen

Peel and core 2 apples, then cut into 1-inch pieces. Heat oil in heavy large pot over medium-high heat. Add shallots; sauté 3 minutes. Add parsnips; sauté 3 minutes. Add apple pieces and coriander; stir 1 minute. Add 5 cups broth; bring to boil. Reduce heat and simmer until vegetables are very tender, about 25 minutes. Cool slightly.

Working in batches, puree soup in blender until smooth, thinning with more broth by 1/2 cupfuls as desired. Return soup to pot; bring to simmer. Season to taste with salt and pepper.

Meanwhile, cut remaining apple (with peel) into thin slices. Ladle soup into bowls. Drizzle soup with yogurt. Fan several apple slices on top and serve.

6 SERVINGS

Onion Soup with Thyme and Cider

    4 tablespoons unsalted butter
    3 tablespoons olive oil
    6 large onions (about 3½ pounds), halved, thinly sliced
    3 cups low-salt chicken broth
  2½ cups bottled apple cider
   12 large thyme sprigs
       Chopped fresh thyme

Melt butter with oil in large pot over medium-high heat. Add onions; sauté until soft and dark brown, about 20 minutes. Add chicken broth, cider, and thyme sprigs. Bring to boil. Reduce heat; season with salt and pepper. Simmer soup, uncovered, 25 minutes. Discard thyme sprigs. *(Soup can be made 1 day ahead. Cool slightly. Chill uncovered until cold, then cover and keep refrigerated. Rewarm over low heat before continuing.)* Divide among 6 soup bowls, garnish with chopped thyme, and serve.

6 SERVINGS

Red Bell Pepper Soup with Orange and Basil

       Nonstick vegetable oil spray
  1½ pounds red bell peppers (about 3 large), quartered, seeded
    1 large yellow bell pepper, quartered, seeded
    1 pound plum tomatoes, trimmed, quartered
    1 cup sliced onion
    3 garlic cloves, thinly sliced
    2 tablespoons olive oil

  1¾ cups (or more) low-salt chicken broth, divided
    3 tablespoons chopped fresh basil, divided
    1 teaspoon grated orange peel

Preheat oven to 425°F. Spray large rimmed baking sheet with nonstick spray. Arrange all bell peppers and tomatoes on sheet, cut side up. Scatter onion and garlic over. Drizzle oil over vegetables; sprinkle with salt and pepper. Roast until peppers are soft and beginning to brown around edges, turning occasionally, about 1 hour. Remove from oven. Enclose yellow pepper in paper bag 10 minutes, then peel and finely chop. Reserve for garnish.

Transfer half of remaining roasted vegetable mixture, 1 cup broth, 1 tablespoon basil, and orange peel to blender and puree until smooth. Transfer to large saucepan. Puree remaining vegetable mixture and ¾ cup broth in blender until smooth. Transfer to same saucepan. Thin soup with additional broth, if desired. Season to taste with salt and pepper. *(Can be prepared 1 day ahead. Cover and refrigerate.)*

Rewarm soup over medium heat, if desired. Ladle hot or chilled soup into 4 bowls. Sprinkle with reserved chopped yellow pepper and remaining 2 tablespoons basil and serve.

4 SERVINGS

Summer Minestrone with Pesto

    3 tablespoons olive oil
    1 medium onion, chopped
    6 cups low-salt chicken broth
    2 carrots, peeled, cut into ½-inch-thick rounds
    2 celery stalks, cut into ½-inch pieces
    4 small red-skinned potatoes, quartered
    ½ pound green beans, trimmed, cut into 1-inch pieces
    3 small zucchini, halved lengthwise, cut into ½-inch pieces
    1 15-ounce can cannellini (white kidney beans), drained
    2 tomatoes, peeled, crushed
    2 cups fresh spinach leaves, chopped
    6 tablespoons purchased pesto
       Freshly grated Parmesan cheese

Heat olive oil in heavy large pot over medium heat. Add onion and sauté until soft, about 4 minutes. Add broth and next 7 ingredients. Increase heat to high and bring soup to boil. Reduce heat to medium-low, partially cover pot, and simmer until potatoes are tender, about 10 minutes. Stir in spinach; simmer 3 minutes longer. Season soup to taste with salt and pepper. Ladle soup into 6 bowls; garnish each with 1 tablespoon pesto. Serve, passing grated Parmesan cheese separately.

6 SERVINGS

Dinner with the Neighbors for 4

Red Bell Pepper Soup with Orange and Basil
(opposite)

Roast Racks of Lamb with New Potatoes and Mint Pesto
(page 62)

Sautéed Spinach

Merlot

Almond Biscotti and Vanilla Ice Cream

Coffee

Chilled Corn and Buttermilk Soup

6 large ears fresh corn, husked

1 tablespoon vegetable oil

½ cup chopped shallots (about 3 large)

2 tablespoons coarsely grated peeled fresh ginger

2 garlic cloves, minced

6 cups low-salt chicken broth

1 cup buttermilk

Additional buttermilk
Chopped fresh chives

Cut corn kernels off cobs; transfer kernels to large bowl. Scrape cobs over bowl with knife to remove any remaining corn and milky liquid. Break cobs in half crosswise and reserve.

Heat oil in heavy large saucepan over medium-high heat. Add shallots, ginger, and garlic; sauté until shallots begin to soften, about 2 minutes. Add corn and any accumulated liquid in bowl. Cook until heated through, stirring occasionally, about 3 minutes. Add cobs and broth. Bring soup to boil; reduce heat to low, cover pan, and simmer until corn is very tender, about 30 minutes. Discard cobs.

Working in batches, puree soup in blender. Transfer to large bowl. Stir 1 cup buttermilk into soup. Cover and refrigerate until chilled, at least 3 hours. (*Can be made 1 day ahead. Keep chilled.*)

Season soup with salt and pepper. Divide soup among 8 bowls. Drizzle with additional buttermilk, sprinkle with chives, and serve.

8 SERVINGS

Summer Evening Supper for 8

Chilled Corn and Buttermilk Soup
(*at left, pictured opposite*)

Barbecued Tri-Tip with Caramelized Red Onions
(*page 50*)

Bibb Lettuce, Watercress, and Radish Salad
(*page 159*)

Grilled Asparagus

Cabernet Sauvignon

Almond and Mixed-Berry Shortcakes
(*page 186*)

Mint and Lemon Iced Tea

16	cups water, divided
2¼	cups sugar
9	large fresh mint sprigs
5	family-size tea bags or 8 to 12 standard-size tea bags
1½	6-ounce cans frozen lemonade concentrate, thawed

Ice cubes

Lemon wedges or slices

Additional fresh mint sprigs

Bring 12 cups water to boil in large pot over high heat. Remove pot from heat. Add sugar, mint, and tea bags; stir until sugar dissolves. Let steep 1 hour. Discard tea bags and mint sprigs. Mix in lemonade concentrate, then remaining 4 cups water. Pour into 2 large pitchers; chill at least 3 hours and up to 1 day.

Serve over ice. Garnish with lemon wedges and mint sprigs.

MAKES ABOUT 18 CUPS

Raspberry Lemonade

2   10-ounce packages frozen sweetened raspberries in syrup, thawed
2   12-ounce cans frozen lemonade concentrate, thawed
9   cups water

   Ice cubes
   Fresh raspberries
   Lemon wedges or slices

Puree raspberries with syrup in processor until smooth. Strain into medium bowl; discard seeds. Pour lemonade concentrate into large pitcher; add 9 cups water. Mix in 1 cup raspberry puree (reserve remaining puree for another use). (*Can be made 1 day ahead. Cover; chill.*)

   Serve over ice, adding fresh raspberries to each glass. Garnish with lemon wedges and serve.

MAKES ABOUT 13 CUPS

Cherry Smash

1   cup fresh pitted Bing cherries
¼   cup kirsch (clear cherry brandy)
¼   cup sugar

1   cup ice cubes
6   tablespoons Courvoisier or other premium Cognac
¼   cup orange curaçao
2   tablespoons fresh lemon juice
1   tablespoon Heering cherry liqueur or other cherry liqueur

Combine cherries, kirsch, and sugar in medium bowl; stir to blend. Let stand at room temperature 24 hours, stirring occasionally. (*Brandied cherries can be made 2 weeks ahead. Cover and chill.*)

   Place 2 Martini glasses in freezer and chill at least 2 hours.

   Place 3 brandied cherries in each of 2 chilled glasses; crush cherries with back of spoon. Combine ice cubes, Cognac, orange curaçao, lemon juice, and cherry liqueur in cocktail shaker. Shake well, strain into Martini glasses with cherries, and serve.

2 SERVINGS

The leftover brandied cherries will keep for up to two weeks in the refrigerator. For an attractive garnish, thread a 4x½-inch strip of orange peel on a short skewer and top with a cherry, then place in drink before serving.

Pear Martini with Lemon and Rosemary

ROSEMARY SYRUP

1 cup sugar

1 cup water

4 4-inch rosemary sprigs

MARTINI

1 750-ml bottle premium vodka

5 tablespoons fresh lemon juice

3 tablespoons poire Williams (clear pear brandy)

12 ice cubes

12 small rosemary sprigs

FOR ROSEMARY SYRUP: Bring sugar and water to boil in small saucepan, stirring to dissolve sugar. Add rosemary sprigs. Reduce heat and simmer 2 minutes. Cool mixture completely. Discard rosemary.

FOR MARTINI: Mix rosemary syrup, vodka, lemon juice, and brandy in large pitcher. Cover pitcher with plastic wrap and place in freezer until mixture is cold, about 3 hours. Remove pitcher from freezer; add ice cubes. Stir briskly to melt ice partially. Strain mixture into chilled Martini glasses. Garnish each glass with rosemary sprig.

12 SERVINGS

Mango Lassi with Cinnamon

1½ cups diced peeled pitted mango (about 1½ large)

1 cup plain nonfat yogurt

1 cup ice cubes

¼ cup low-fat (1%) milk

1½ tablespoons honey

½ teaspoon vanilla extract

¼ teaspoon ground cinnamon

⅛ teaspoon ground cardamom

2 mango wedges or slices (for garnish)

Combine diced mango, yogurt, 1 cup ice cubes, milk, honey, vanilla extract, ground cinnamon, and ground cardamom in blender. Puree until smooth. Pour smoothie into 2 glasses. Garnish each glass with mango wedge and serve.

2 SERVINGS

Spiced Hot Chocolate

  6 cups whole milk

 ¾ cup (packed) dark brown sugar

15 whole cardamom pods, crushed

12 whole cloves

  2 cinnamon sticks, broken in half

  2 whole star anise*

 ¾ teaspoon whole coriander seeds

 ¾ teaspoon ground nutmeg

 ¼ teaspoon dried crushed red pepper

 ½ cup unsweetened cocoa powder

 ¾ teaspoon vanilla extract

Bring first 9 ingredients to simmer in heavy large saucepan, stirring until sugar dissolves. Remove from heat, cover, and let steep 20 minutes. Add cocoa powder and vanilla. Bring to simmer, whisking until blended. Strain hot chocolate into 8-cup measuring cup; discard spices. Divide hot chocolate among 6 mugs.

Brown star-shaped seedpods sold in some supermarkets, specialty foods stores, and Asian markets.

6 SERVINGS

Ginger Passion Fruit Coolers

1 6- to 7-inch-long piece fresh ginger, peeled
2½ cups vodka
2 cups nonalcoholic ginger beer
2 cups frozen concentrated passion fruit juice cocktail, thawed

Ice cubes
Fresh mint sprigs

An effervescent combination of vodka, ginger beer (found at many liquor stores), and passion fruit juice. Swizzle sticks fashioned out of fresh ginger are a fun touch.

Cut ginger lengthwise into ¼-inch-thick slices. Cut slices lengthwise into ¼-inch-thick sticks, making at least 8. Combine vodka, ginger beer, and juice concentrate in pitcher. *(Ginger sticks and vodka mixture can be made 1 day ahead. Cover separately and chill.)*

Divide vodka mixture among Martini glasses. Add ice cubes and ginger stick to each; garnish with mint.

8 SERVINGS

Classic Champagne Cocktail

6 sugar cubes
¼ cup brandy
Angostura bitters
1 750-ml bottle Champagne or sparkling wine
6 1½x¼-inch strips orange peel

Place 1 sugar cube in each of 6 Champagne flutes. Add 2 teaspoons brandy, then 6 drops bitters to each glass. Divide Champagne among glasses. Garnish with orange peel and serve.

6 SERVINGS

Watermelon and Strawberry Smoothie

6 cups ½-inch cubes seeded watermelon, divided
1 pint strawberry sorbet, divided
Fresh strawberries

Combine 3 cups watermelon and half of sorbet in blender. Blend until mixture is smooth, about 1 minute. Transfer mixture to pitcher. Repeat with remaining watermelon and sorbet. Divide smoothie among 4 glasses. Garnish with fresh berries and serve immediately.

4 SERVINGS

Moroccan Chicken with
Eggplant, Tomatoes, and
Almonds (page 82)

Main Courses

Meats

Poultry

Seafood

Meatless

Pasta & Pizza

Braised Orange-Ginger Short Ribs with Dried Apricots

4 large oranges
¾ cup hoisin sauce*
⅓ cup tomato paste
2 garlic cloves, minced
1 2-inch piece fresh ginger, peeled, cut crosswise into thin slices

12 3- to 4-inch-long meaty beef short ribs (about 4½ pounds), top membrane trimmed
24 dried apricots
Chopped fresh parsley

Preheat oven to 300°F. Using vegetable peeler, remove four 4x1-inch strips from rind of 1 orange. Grate peel from 2 more oranges. Cut 4 oranges in half; squeeze out 1¼ cups juice. Whisk grated orange peel, orange juice, hoisin sauce, tomato paste, and garlic in large bowl to blend. Stir in ginger.

Sprinkle ribs with salt and pepper. Place in heavy large ovenproof pot. Pour orange-ginger mixture over ribs. Stir in orange strips and apricots. Cover and bake 2 hours. Stir rib mixture; reduce oven temperature to 250°F. Continue cooking ribs, covered, until meat is very tender, about 1 hour longer. *(Can be made 1 day ahead. Cool. Refrigerate uncovered until cold, then cover and refrigerate. Spoon off solidified fat, then rewarm ribs over medium heat before serving.)* Using slotted spoon, transfer ribs and apricots to large platter. Spoon off any fat from sauce in pot. Pour sauce over ribs. Sprinkle with parsley and serve.

Available in the Asian foods section of many supermarkets and at Asian markets.

6 SERVINGS

MEATS

Seared New York Steaks with Arugula Salad and Saint André Cheese

5 green onions; 1 minced, 4 coarsely chopped
3 tablespoons balsamic vinegar
1 tablespoon Dijon mustard
½ cup olive oil

8 1-inch-thick New York steaks (each 10 to 12 ounces)
Additional olive oil
Coarse sea salt
Coarsely cracked black pepper

2 5-ounce bags baby arugula

14 ounces Saint André triple-cream cheese or other soft creamy cheese, cut into 16 wedges

Wedges of Saint André, a decadent triple-cream cheese from France, transform steak and salad into a simply elegant entrée.

Whisk minced green onion, vinegar, and mustard in small bowl. Gradually whisk in ½ cup oil. Season dressing with salt and pepper. *(Can be made 2 hours ahead. Cover and let stand at room temperature.)*

Preheat oven to 400°F. Brush both sides of steaks with olive oil. Sprinkle with sea salt and cracked pepper. Heat 2 large ovenproof skillets over medium-high heat. Add 4 steaks to each skillet and sear 2 minutes per side. Transfer skillets to oven and roast steaks, without turning, until cooked to desired doneness, about 8 minutes for medium-rare.

Meanwhile, combine arugula and 4 chopped green onions in large bowl. Add dressing; toss. Divide salad among plates.

Thinly slice steaks crosswise. Arrange 1 steak, slices fanned out slightly, and 2 cheese wedges alongside arugula salad on each plate.

8 SERVINGS

Cheeseburgers with Charred Green Chiles and Onions

½ cup mayonnaise
½ cup prepared barbecue sauce

2¼ pounds freshly ground beef chuck
1 teaspoon salt
½ teaspoon ground black pepper

3 metal skewers
3 ½-inch-thick onion slices
Vegetable oil
3 poblano chiles*

12 thin slices cheddar cheese, room temperature
6 onion rolls or sesame-seed hamburger buns, split

Whisk mayonnaise and barbecue sauce in small bowl to blend. Cover and chill.

Mix ground chuck with 1 teaspoon salt and ½ teaspoon pepper just to blend (do not overmix). Form mixture into six 1½-inch-thick patties. Cover and let stand at room temperature 30 minutes.

Prepare barbecue (medium-high heat). Run 1 metal skewer horizontally through center of each onion slice. Brush onion slices lightly with oil to coat. Rub chiles with oil. Transfer onions and chiles to barbecue. Grill onions until softened and browned, about 5 minutes per side. Remove skewers from onions. Chop onions; transfer to small bowl. Char chiles until blackened on all sides. Enclose chiles in paper bag 10 minutes. Peel, seed, and chop chiles. Mix into onions. Season onions and chiles to taste with salt and pepper.

Sprinkle burgers with salt and pepper. Grill until cooked to desired doneness, about 4 minutes per side for medium. Top each burger with 2 cheese slices during last minute of cooking. Place bottom halves of rolls on work surface. Divide chile-onion mixture among rolls. Place cheeseburgers atop chile-onion mixture. Spread 1 tablespoon mayonnaise-barbecue sauce over cheese, cover with bun tops, and serve, passing remaining sauce.

Fresh green chiles, often called pasillas, *sold at some supermarkets and Latin American markets.*

MAKES 6

Fricassee of Beef and Fava Beans

5 pounds fresh fava beans, shelled, or 5 cups frozen double-peeled fava beans
(from two 16-ounce packages), thawed

2 tablespoons butter, divided
2 tablespoons olive oil, divided
1 1½-pound piece beef tenderloin, cut in half lengthwise, then crosswise into
½-inch-thick slices

2 large onions, finely chopped

½ cup whipping cream
¼ cup fresh lemon juice
2 large egg yolks
2 teaspoons salt
1 teaspoon ground black pepper
2 tablespoons chopped fresh mint

Cook fresh fava beans in large pot of boiling salted water 2 minutes. Drain favas. Place in large bowl of ice water. Drain. Slip outer skin off each bean and discard skin; place beans in large bowl. (If using frozen beans, do not blanch.)

Melt 1 tablespoon butter with 1 tablespoon oil in large nonstick skillet over high heat. Working in batches, add beef and sauté just until browned on both sides, about 2 minutes. Transfer beef to medium bowl.

Melt remaining 1 tablespoon butter with 1 tablespoon oil in same skillet over medium heat. Add onions; sauté until tender and golden, about 15 minutes. Add fava beans; sauté 5 minutes. Remove from heat; cool 15 minutes.

Meanwhile, whisk cream, lemon juice, yolks, salt, and pepper in small bowl to blend. Stir into fava bean mixture. Cook over medium-low heat just until sauce thickens slightly and is heated through, about 6 minutes (do not boil). Add beef and stir until heated through, about 3 minutes. Transfer to rimmed platter. Sprinkle with mint.

6 SERVINGS

A fusion of flavors and technique from two cuisines makes this main course taste new. The cooking method is based on an Italian *fricassea* made with egg yolks and cream; the combination of favas and mint is Middle Eastern. The resulting dish is absolutely delicious. Serve with plenty of crusty bread to mop up the sauce.

Roast Beef Tenderloin with Merlot and Shallots

¼ cup (½ stick) unsalted butter
½ cup chopped shallots
1½ teaspoons minced fresh thyme
2 tablespoons all purpose flour
1½ cups Merlot or other dry red wine
1½ cups beef broth
1 teaspoon tomato paste

2 2½-pound thick-end beef tenderloin roasts, trimmed
Olive oil

At the market, ask the butcher to trim the beef fat and tendons. At the table, uncork your favorite Cabernet Sauvignon.

Melt butter in medium saucepan over medium-high heat. Add shallots and thyme; sauté until shallots are browned, about 5 minutes. Mix in flour; cook until flour browns, stirring often, about 2 minutes. Whisk in wine and broth. Boil until thick enough to coat spoon, whisking often, about 12 minutes. Whisk in tomato paste; season with salt and pepper. *(Can be made 2 days ahead. Cover; chill.)*

Preheat oven to 450°F. Arrange roasts on rimmed baking sheet. Brush oil over; sprinkle with salt and pepper. Roast until thermometer inserted into center registers 125°F for rare, about 38 minutes. Transfer to platter; let stand 20 minutes.

Add any juices from baking sheet to sauce and bring to simmer. Transfer sauce to bowl. Cut roasts into ¹/₂-inch-thick slices and serve with sauce.

8 SERVINGS

Barbecued Tri-Tip with Caramelized Red Onions

CARAMELIZED RED ONIONS

- 2 tablespoons (¼ stick) butter
- 2 tablespoons olive oil
- 2½ pounds red onions (about 4 medium), halved, thinly sliced
- 2 teaspoons balsamic vinegar
- ½ teaspoon coarse kosher salt
- ¼ teaspoon ground black pepper
- ¼ cup chopped fresh chives

TRI-TIP

- 1 teaspoon garlic powder
- 1 teaspoon salt
- ½ teaspoon ground black pepper
- 2 1½- to 1¾-pound beef loin tri-tip roasts, trimmed of all but ¼ inch of fat
- 2 tablespoons olive oil

  Red Wine Barbecue Sauce (see recipe)

FOR CARAMELIZED RED ONIONS: Melt butter with olive oil in large nonstick skillet over medium heat. Add onions and cook until deep golden brown, stirring frequently, about 30 minutes. Stir in vinegar, 1/2 teaspoon salt, and 1/4 teaspoon pepper. Remove from heat. *(Can be prepared 1 day ahead. Cover and refrigerate. Rewarm over medium heat before serving.)* Stir in chives.

FOR TRI-TIP: Prepare barbecue (medium heat). Mix garlic powder, 1 teaspoon salt, and 1/2 teaspoon pepper in small bowl. Brush both sides of tri-tips with oil and sprinkle with garlic-powder mixture, pressing to adhere. Grill tri-tips 5 minutes per side. Reduce heat to medium-low, or if using charcoal grill, move meat to cooler side of grill. Cover and grill until thermometer inserted into thickest part of meat registers 125°F to 130°F for medium-rare, brushing with Red Wine Barbecue Sauce and turning every 10 minutes, about 30 minutes longer.

Transfer tri-tips to work surface; let stand 10 minutes. Cut meat crosswise into very thin slices; arrange on platter. Surround with caramelized onions and serve.

8 SERVINGS

Slicing this sturdy cut of beef very thinly after grilling makes it more tender. Pour a California Zinfandel or a cold pale ale.

Red Wine Barbecue Sauce

- 1 tablespoon olive oil
- 1 large garlic clove, minced
- 1/4 teaspoon ground cumin
- 1/4 teaspoon ground chipotle chile pepper powder*
- 1/3 cup dry red wine
- 1/2 cup ketchup
- 1 tablespoon apple cider vinegar
- 1 tablespoon soy sauce
- 1/8 teaspoon liquid smoke**

This sauce is basted on the meat as it grills. It is also great served alongside; the recipe doubles easily.

Heat oil in heavy medium saucepan over medium heat. Add garlic, cumin, and chipotle chile powder; stir 1 minute. Add wine and simmer 2 minutes. Stir in ketchup, vinegar, soy sauce, and liquid smoke; simmer 2 minutes longer. *(Can be made 2 days ahead. Cover and chill.)*

Available in the spice section of most supermarkets.
**A smoke-flavored liquid seasoning available at many supermarkets and specialty foods stores.*

MAKES ABOUT 1 CUP

Pepper-Crusted Steaks with Worcestershire Sauce

4 14- to 16-ounce New York strip steaks
   (each about 1 to 1¼ inches thick)
3 tablespoons black peppercorns, cracked
   with mallet
2 teaspoons coarse kosher salt

½ cup plus 2 tablespoons (1¼ sticks)
   butter
4 teaspoons Worcestershire sauce
1½ teaspoons balsamic vinegar
1 pound portobello mushrooms, cut into
   ⅓-inch-thick slices

Sprinkle steaks with cracked peppercorns and coarse salt. Let steaks stand at room temperature 30 minutes.

Melt ½ cup butter in large skillet over medium heat. Stir in Worcestershire sauce and vinegar. Stir in mushrooms. Sprinkle with salt. Remove from heat.

Prepare barbecue (medium-high heat). Grill steaks until cooked to desired doneness, about 5 minutes per side for medium-rare. Transfer to plates. Top each steak with ½ tablespoon butter. Tent with foil. Grill mushrooms until soft and beginning to release juices, about 3 minutes per side. Divide mushrooms among steaks and serve.

4 TO 6 SERVINGS

Sesame-Ginger Beef and Asparagus Stir-Fry

1   pound lean top sirloin, sliced into thin strips
2   teaspoons cornstarch

4   tablespoons peanut oil or vegetable oil, divided

1   teaspoon oriental sesame oil
1   pound thin asparagus, trimmed, cut on diagonal into 1½-inch pieces
1   small bunch green onions, cut on diagonal into 1½-inch pieces
1½ tablespoons minced peeled fresh ginger
⅔   cup beef broth
1   tablespoon fish sauce (nam pla or nuoc nam)*
1   teaspoon sugar

Combine beef and cornstarch in large bowl. Using hands, rub cornstarch into beef to coat well.

Heat 2 tablespoons peanut oil in large skillet over high heat. Working in batches, add beef in single layer and cook, undisturbed, until meat begins to blacken on bottom, about 1½ minutes. Turn; cook until second side browns, about 1 minute. Transfer to large plate.

Heat remaining 2 tablespoons peanut oil and 1 teaspoon sesame oil in same skillet over medium-high heat. Add asparagus, green onions, and ginger; sauté until vegetables are tinged brown and crisp-tender, about 2 minutes. Add broth, fish sauce, and sugar; bring to boil. Return beef to skillet and cook until sauce is slightly thickened, about 1 minute. Transfer to platter and serve.

Fish sauce is available in the Asian foods section of many supermarkets and at Asian markets.

4 SERVINGS

Roast New York Strip Loin with Adobo Rub

Adobo—a paste prepared with chiles, spices, and vinegar or sometimes citrus juice— is a flavoring agent found throughout the Spanish-speaking world. This variation with paprika and rosemary serves as the seasoning rub for the meat.

      6 large garlic cloves, peeled
    ¼ cup Spanish sweet paprika
    ¼ cup red wine vinegar
      2 tablespoons olive oil
      1 tablespoon chopped fresh rosemary
      2 teaspoons salt
      1 teaspoon freshly ground black pepper
      1 6-pound New York strip loin, all but ½ inch fat trimmed

Chop garlic in processor. Add paprika, vinegar, oil, rosemary, salt, and pepper; grind to thick paste. Rub all over New York strip loin. Wrap loin in plastic; chill overnight.

Preheat oven to 450°F. Place large metal rack in roasting pan. Uncover meat and arrange, fat side up, on rack. Roast meat 15 minutes. Reduce oven temperature to 350°F. Continue roasting meat until thermometer inserted into center registers 125°F for rare, about 40 minutes longer. Cover meat loosely with aluminum foil and let rest 20 minutes. Transfer to platter. Cut into ½-inch-thick slices and serve.

12 SERVINGS

Chili with Sausage and Jalapeño

- 4 tablespoons olive oil, divided
- 1 pound lean ground beef
- ¾ pound Italian sweet sausages, casings removed
- 1 large onion, chopped
- 1 large green bell pepper, chopped
- 2 jalapeño chiles, seeded, finely chopped
- 2 bay leaves
- 6 garlic cloves, minced
- 2 28-ounce cans crushed tomatoes with added puree
- 3 tablespoons chili powder
- 2 tablespoons ground cumin
- 2 tablespoons (packed) golden brown sugar
- 1 tablespoon ground black pepper
- 2 teaspoons dried oregano
- 2 teaspoons dried basil
-   Pinch of cayenne pepper
- 2 tablespoons fresh lime juice
-   Hot pepper sauce
-   Grated Monterey Jack cheese
-   Chopped red onion
-   Sour cream

Heat 2 tablespoons oil in heavy large pot over high heat. Add beef and sausages; cook until brown, breaking up with spoon, about 8 minutes. Transfer meat mixture to bowl. Reduce heat to medium-high. Add remaining oil to pot. Add onion, bell pepper, jalapeños, and bay leaves. Cook until vegetables are soft, stirring frequently, about 7 minutes. Add garlic; sauté 1 minute. Return meat to pot. Mix in tomatoes and next 7 ingredients. Simmer 25 minutes, stirring occasionally. Mix in lime juice. Season with salt. Serve chili in bowls, passing hot sauce, cheese, red onion, and sour cream separately.

8 SERVINGS

Veal Paprikash

- 3 tablespoons (or more) lard, or 1 tablespoon bacon fat and 2 tablespoons (or more) olive oil
- 2 cups thinly sliced onions
- 1 large shallot, minced

- 2½ pounds ¼-inch-thick veal scallops
- ½ cup canned diced tomatoes in juice
- 1 tablespoon Hungarian sweet paprika

½ teaspoon Hungarian hot paprika or cayenne pepper
1 teaspoon dried marjoram
½ cup sour cream

Melt lard in heavy large skillet over medium heat. Add onions; cover skillet and cook until onions are soft, stirring occasionally, about 10 minutes. Add shallot; increase heat to medium-high and sauté until onions are golden, about 5 minutes. Using slotted spoon, transfer onions and shallot to small bowl.

Sprinkle veal with salt and pepper. Working in batches, add veal scallops to drippings in skillet and sauté until browned, about 1 minute per side, adding more lard as needed and transferring veal to plate after each batch. Return onion mixture to skillet. Add tomatoes with juice, sweet paprika, hot paprika, and marjoram. Simmer 5 minutes, stirring constantly. Return veal and any accumulated juices to sauce. Simmer 1 minute, turning veal to coat. Using slotted spoon, transfer veal to platter. Mix sour cream into sauce and heat through (do not boil). Season sauce to taste with salt and pepper. Pour over veal and serve.

8 SERVINGS

Veal Chops with Rosemary Butter

¼ cup (½ stick) unsalted butter, room temperature
2½ teaspoons minced fresh rosemary, divided
1 teaspoon chopped fresh thyme, divided
   Pinch of salt

4 12-ounce veal rib chops, each about 1 inch thick
4 tablespoons olive oil, divided

1 4-inch-long fresh rosemary sprig
1 garlic clove, flattened
3 tablespoons dry white wine
3 tablespoons low-salt chicken broth

Whisk butter, 1 teaspoon rosemary, ¼ teaspoon thyme, and pinch of salt in small bowl to blend. Wrap rosemary butter in plastic wrap, forming 1½-inch-diameter log. Chill at least 2 hours. (*Can be made 1 week ahead. Keep refrigerated.*)

Arrange chops in single layer in large baking dish. Drizzle with 2 tablespoons olive oil. Sprinkle with remaining 1½ teaspoons rosemary and ¾ teaspoon thyme. Sprinkle with salt and pepper. Rub oil and seasonings into chops. (*Can be prepared 1 day ahead. Cover with plastic wrap and chill. Let stand at room temperature 1 hour before continuing.*)

Heat 2 tablespoons olive oil in heavy large skillet over medium-high heat. Add rosemary sprig and garlic. Sauté until garlic is fragrant but not brown, about 2 minutes. Discard rosemary sprig and garlic. Increase heat to high. Add chops; cook until chops are browned and meat thermometer inserted horizontally into center reads 130°F, about 2 minutes per side. Transfer chops to plate. Pour off drippings from pan. Reduce heat to medium-high. Add wine to skillet and cook until reduced to about 2 teaspoons, scraping up browned bits, about 30 seconds. Add chicken broth; cook until reduced to about 2 tablespoons, about 30 seconds. Drizzle over chops.

Cut rosemary butter into 4 slices. Place 1 slice atop each veal chop and serve immediately.

4 SERVINGS

Saturday Night Dinner for 4

Dilled Gravlax with Mustard Sauce
(*page 22*)

Champagne

Veal Chops with Rosemary Butter
(*at left, pictured opposite*)

Pancetta Green Beans
(*page 145*)

Lemon-Barley Pilaf
(*page 147*)

Burgundy

Chocolate-Amaretti Tortes
(*page 204*)

Veal Stew with Green Olives and Potatoes

½ cup all purpose flour

1 teaspoon salt

¼ teaspoon ground black pepper

1½ pounds veal stew meat, cut into ¾-inch pieces

2½ tablespoons (or more) olive oil, divided

2 medium onions, coarsely chopped

2 large carrots, peeled, sliced

2 garlic cloves, minced

½ cup dry red wine

1 14½-ounce can whole tomatoes in juice

½ cup (or more) water

3 3x½-inch strips orange peel, cut into thin slivers

1 pound Yukon Gold potatoes, peeled, cut into 1-inch cubes

¼ cup coarsely chopped pitted brine-cured green olives

Combine first 4 ingredients in 1-gallon resealable plastic bag. Shake to coat veal. Remove veal; shake off excess flour. Heat 1 tablespoon oil in large nonstick skillet over medium-high heat. Add veal; sauté until brown, adding 1 tablespoon oil to skillet as needed, about 5 minutes. Transfer veal to 6-quart slow cooker. Add ½ tablespoon oil, then onions and carrots to skillet. Sauté 8 minutes. Add garlic; stir 1 minute. Transfer vegetables to slow cooker.

Add wine to skillet; boil until reduced by ⅓, about 1 minute. Pour wine over veal. Add next 3 ingredients. Cover and cook until meat is tender, adding more water by ¼ cupfuls if mixture is dry, about 4 hours. Season with salt and pepper.

Cook potatoes in large saucepan of boiling salted water until tender, about 15 minutes. Drain. Divide potatoes among 4 bowls. Top with stew. Sprinkle with olives.

4 SERVINGS

Grilled Leg of Lamb with Mustard and Rosemary

1 tablespoon dry mustard

1 teaspoon ground cardamom

¼ teaspoon ground cloves

1 tablespoon apple cider vinegar

½ cup frozen apple juice concentrate, thawed

½ cup spicy brown mustard (such as Gulden's)

1 tablespoon chopped fresh rosemary

2 teaspoons olive oil

Coarse kosher salt

1 5-pound boneless leg of lamb, butterflied, trimmed of all fat

Nonstick vegetable oil spray

Combine first 3 ingredients in small bowl. Gradually whisk in vinegar. Let stand 15 minutes. Whisk in apple juice concentrate, brown mustard, rosemary, and oil. Season marinade with coarse salt and pepper.

Place lamb, boned side up, in 15x10x2-inch glass baking dish. Sprinkle with salt and pepper. Spread 1/3 cup marinade over top to coat. Turn over. Sprinkle with salt and pepper. Spread remaining marinade over lamb. Cover dish with plastic wrap; chill overnight.

Spray grill rack with nonstick spray. Prepare barbecue (medium heat). Place lamb on grill with marinade still clinging (reserve dish with marinade). Grill 15 minutes. Turn lamb over. Grill 15 minutes, brushing with marinade from reserved dish. Turn lamb over again and grill until thermometer inserted into thickest part registers 130°F for medium-rare, brushing often with any remaining marinade, about 5 minutes longer per side. Transfer lamb to platter. Cover loosely with foil; let rest 15 minutes. Slice lamb thinly; arrange on platter and serve.

Start marinating the lamb one day before you plan to serve it.

8 SERVINGS

Spiced Lamb Chops with Mint-Mango Sauce

MINT-MANGO SAUCE

- 2 1-pound ripe mangoes, peeled, seeded
- 2 cups fresh mint leaves
- 4 green onions, cut into 1-inch pieces
- 2 tablespoons fresh lime juice
- 2 serrano chiles, halved, seeded

LAMB CHOPS

- 1½ tablespoons ground cumin
- 1½ tablespoons ground coriander
- 1 tablespoon coarse kosher salt
- 1½ teaspoons ground cinnamon
- 1 teaspoon turmeric
- ½ teaspoon cayenne pepper
- ½ teaspoon ground cardamom
- ⅛ teaspoon ground cloves
- ¼ cup olive oil
- 2 garlic cloves, chopped
- 16 1-inch-thick lamb loin chops
  Fresh mint sprigs

FOR MINT-MANGO SAUCE: Blend all ingredients in processor until smooth. Transfer to small bowl. Season with salt. Cover and chill. (*Can be made 1 day ahead.*)

FOR LAMB CHOPS: Prepare barbecue (medium-high heat). Whisk first 8 ingredients in small bowl. Mix oil and garlic in another bowl. Brush chops on both sides with oil mixture, then press chops into spice mixture to coat both sides. Grill chops to desired doneness, about 4 minutes per side for medium-rare. Transfer to platter. Garnish with mint sprigs. Serve warm or at room temperature with sauce.

8 SERVINGS

Hunan Lamb Chops

- ⅓ cup hoisin sauce*
- 2 tablespoons soy sauce
- 2 tablespoons dry Sherry
- 2 teaspoons chili oil
- 1 tablespoon rice vinegar
- 3 large garlic cloves, finely chopped
- ½ cup thinly sliced green onions, divided
- 8 ½-inch-thick shoulder lamb chops (about 2 pounds total)

Prepare barbecue (high heat). Whisk hoisin sauce, soy sauce, Sherry, chili oil, rice vinegar, and finely chopped garlic to blend in shallow dish; mix in 1/3 cup thinly sliced green onions. Add lamb and turn to coat. Let marinate 20 minutes.

Brush grill rack with oil. Grill lamb to desired doneness, about 3 minutes per side for medium-rare. Place 2 lamb chops on each plate. Sprinkle lamb with remaining green onions and serve.

Hoisin sauce is available in the Asian foods section of many supermarkets and at Asian markets.

4 SERVINGS

Lamb Loin Chops with Artichokes and Rosemary

    3 tablespoons olive oil, divided
    3 garlic cloves, minced, divided
 3½ teaspoons minced fresh rosemary, divided
    2 teaspoons grated orange peel, divided
    2 8-ounce packages frozen artichoke hearts, thawed
 1½ cups low-salt chicken broth

    8 1-inch-thick loin lamb chops

Heat 2 tablespoons oil in large skillet over medium-high heat. Add 2 minced garlic cloves, 2 teaspoons rosemary, and 1/2 teaspoon orange peel; stir 30 seconds. Add artichoke hearts and broth; bring to boil. Cover; boil 5 minutes. Uncover; cook until sauce thickens, stirring occasionally, about 4 minutes. Remove from heat.

Sprinkle lamb with remaining garlic and rosemary, then salt and pepper. Heat remaining oil in another large skillet over medium-high heat. Add lamb; sauté until cooked to desired doneness, about 4 minutes per side for medium-rare. Transfer lamb to platter.

Spoon off fat from skillet with lamb. Add artichoke mixture; boil 2 minutes, scraping up browned bits. Season with salt and pepper. Spoon artichoke mixture around lamb. Sprinkle with remaining orange peel and serve.

4 SERVINGS

Fireside Supper for 4

Egg Ribbon and Parmesan Soup
(page 29)

Lamb Loin Chops with Artichokes and Rosemary
(at left)

Rice Pilaf

Merlot

Quick Apple Tart
(page 173)

Roast Racks of Lamb with New Potatoes and Mint Pesto

LAMB

- ½ cup plus 1 tablespoon olive oil
- 6 garlic cloves, minced
- 2 tablespoons Dijon mustard
- 1¾ pounds unpeeled new red-skinned potatoes (about 22 1½-inch-diameter), scrubbed, quartered
- 2 racks of lamb (about 1¼ to 1½ pounds each), trimmed, frenched

PESTO

- 2 cups (packed) fresh mint leaves
- ¾ cup olive oil
- ¼ cup fresh lemon juice
- 4 garlic cloves
- 1 teaspoon salt
- ½ teaspoon dried crushed red pepper

Fresh mint sprigs

FOR LAMB: Whisk ½ cup oil, garlic, and mustard in small bowl to blend. Transfer ⅓ cup mustard mixture to large bowl; add potatoes and toss to coat. Brush remaining mustard mixture over lamb. Transfer to large rimmed baking sheet.

FOR PESTO: Puree all ingredients except mint sprigs in processor.

Preheat oven to 425°F. Heat 1 tablespoon oil in large skillet over medium-high heat. Add 1 lamb rack, rounded side down, and cook until brown, about 3 minutes. Return to baking sheet. Repeat with remaining lamb rack. Let stand until cool enough to handle, about 10 minutes. Arrange racks facing each other, bone ends up and brown sides out, about 2 inches apart on same baking sheet; tip toward each other, intertwining bones loosely. Scatter potatoes around lamb.

Roast lamb and potatoes until thermometer inserted into center of lamb registers 130°F for medium-rare, about 20 minutes. Transfer lamb to platter and tent with foil. Continue roasting potatoes until cooked through and crisp, stirring once, about 15 minutes longer. Surround lamb with potatoes, garnish with mint sprigs, and serve with pesto.

4 SERVINGS

Wine-Braised Lamb Shanks with Herbes de Provence

5   tablespoons olive oil, divided

2   large leeks (white and pale green parts only), chopped (about 2½ cups)

6   large whole garlic cloves

6   large lamb shanks (12 to 14 ounces each)
     All purpose flour

2⅔ cups dry red wine

1   cup canned crushed tomatoes with added puree

¼   ounce dried porcini mushrooms

1½ tablespoons dried herbes de Provence

1¼ pounds slender carrots, peeled, cut diagonally into ½-inch-long pieces

½   cup chopped fresh parsley

Heat 1 tablespoon oil in heavy wide pot over medium heat. Add leeks and garlic; sauté until leeks soften, about 5 minutes. Transfer leek mixture to small bowl.

Sprinkle lamb shanks with salt and pepper; dust with flour to coat. Heat remaining 4 tablespoons oil in same pot over medium-high heat. Add lamb and cook until brown, turning occasionally, about 12 minutes. Add leek mixture, wine, tomatoes with puree, mushrooms, herbes de Provence, and carrots. Stir to coat lamb with vegetable mixture. Reduce heat to medium-low, cover, and simmer until lamb is very tender, turning twice, about 1 hour 30 minutes. Uncover and continue to simmer until sauce reduces slightly, about 10 minutes longer. Spoon off fat from pan juices. Season lamb to taste with salt and pepper. (*Can be made 1 day ahead. Cool slightly. Chill uncovered until cold, then cover and keep refrigerated. Rewarm, covered, over low heat before serving.*)

Sprinkle with parsley and serve.

6 SERVINGS

If an *herbes de Provence* blend isn't available, use a combination of dried thyme, basil, savory, and fennel seeds. Dried porcini can be found at many supermarkets, Italian markets, and specialty foods stores.

Five-Spice Pork Stir-Fry with Soba Noodles

1 6-ounce package soba noodles or other thin noodles

½ pound ⅓-inch-thick boneless center-cut pork chops, cut crosswise into thin strips

1 teaspoon Chinese five-spice powder*

3 tablespoons peanut oil, divided

2 tablespoons soy sauce

1½ tablespoons unseasoned rice vinegar

1 cup thinly sliced green onions

¾ cup thinly sliced small radishes

Cook noodles in large pot of boiling salted water until almost tender but still firm to bite. Drain well, then return to pot.

Meanwhile, sprinkle pork with salt, pepper, and five-spice powder. Heat 1 tablespoon oil in medium skillet over high heat. Add pork and stir-fry until cooked through, about 2 minutes. Add remaining 2 tablespoons oil, soy sauce, and vinegar; stir 30 seconds.

Add pork, green onions, and radishes to noodles and toss to combine. Season to taste with salt and pepper.

A spice blend that usually contains ground anise, cinnamon, star anise, cloves, and ginger, available in the spice section of most supermarkets.

2 SERVINGS

Grilled Chipotle-Stuffed Pork Tenderloin

2 15-ounce pork tenderloins

2 tablespoons finely chopped canned chipotle chiles, plus 1 tablespoon adobo sauce*

⅓ cup plain whole-milk yogurt

1 tablespoon olive oil

1 tablespoon cumin seeds

Purchased guacamole

Prepare barbecue (medium heat).

Place tenderloins on work surface. Starting at 1 long side, cut each horizontally to within ½ inch of opposite side. Open like book and sprinkle with salt. Spread 1 tablespoon chopped chiles down center of each tenderloin. Close tenderloins, pressing to adhere, and sprinkle with salt.

Whisk yogurt, 1 tablespoon oil, cumin, and 1 tablespoon adobo sauce in small bowl to blend. Transfer tenderloins to plate and brush each heavily with some yogurt sauce. Set tenderloins aside 15 minutes.

Brush grill rack with oil. Grill tenderloins, brushing occasionally with remaining yogurt sauce, until just cooked through and thermometer inserted into thickest part of meat registers 145°F, about 10 minutes per side. Transfer tenderloins to platter. Let stand 5 minutes, then cut crosswise into ½-inch-thick slices. Serve tenderloins with guacamole.

Chipotle chiles canned in a spicy tomato sauce, sometimes called adobo, are sold at some supermarkets, Latin American markets, and specialty foods stores.

4 SERVINGS

Pork Tenderloin with Roasted Apples and Onions

1   large pork tenderloin (about 14 ounces)

3   tablespoons olive oil, divided
2   tablespoons whole grain Dijon mustard
2   teaspoons fennel seeds
1   large onion, sliced
2   medium Granny Smith apples, peeled, cored, sliced ¼ inch thick

½   cup dry white wine or apple cider

Preheat oven to 450°F. Season pork with salt and pepper.

Heat 2 tablespoons oil in large nonstick ovenproof skillet over medium-high heat. Add pork and sear until all sides are brown, turning occasionally, about 5 minutes. Transfer pork to plate. Cool slightly. Spread mustard over top and sides of pork; press fennel seeds into mustard. Add 1 tablespoon oil to skillet. Add onion slices and apples; sauté over medium heat until golden, about 5 minutes. Spread evenly in skillet and sprinkle with salt and pepper. Place pork atop apple-onion mixture.

Transfer skillet to oven and roast until apple-onion mixture is soft and brown and meat thermometer inserted into center of pork registers 150°F, about 15 minutes. Transfer pork to platter and tent with foil. Let stand 5 minutes.

Meanwhile, pour white wine over apple-onion mixture in skillet. Stir mixture over high heat until slightly reduced, about 2 minutes. Cut pork on diagonal into ½-inch-thick slices. Spoon apple-onion mixture onto plates. Top with pork and serve.

4 SERVINGS

Pork Tenderloin with Cider Jus and Rutabaga Puree

    2 cups apple cider
    1 cup low-salt chicken broth
  ¾ cup chopped onion
    6 whole allspice
    3 whole star anise*
    3 large fresh thyme sprigs
    2 cinnamon sticks
    2 teaspoons apple cider vinegar
    1 Turkish bay leaf
    5 tablespoons unsalted butter, cut into ½-inch cubes

    2 12-ounce pork tenderloins, well trimmed
        Olive oil

        Rutabaga Puree (see recipe)

Mix first 9 ingredients in heavy medium saucepan. Boil until mixture is reduced to 1½ cups, about 20 minutes. Strain, pressing on solids to extract liquid. Discard solids. Return liquid to saucepan and boil until reduced to ½ cup, about 3 minutes. Whisk in butter a few pieces at a time. Season with salt and pepper.

Meanwhile, prepare barbecue (medium-high heat). Brush pork with olive oil. Sprinkle generously with salt and pepper. Grill until instant-read thermometer inserted into center of pork registers 145°F, turning frequently, about 20 minutes. Let pork rest 5 minutes (temperature will increase to 150°F). Thinly slice pork crosswise.

Divide pork slices among 6 plates. Spoon Rutabaga Puree alongside. Drizzle sauce over pork and serve immediately.

Brown star-shaped seedpods available in the spice section of some supermarkets and at Asian markets and specialty foods stores.

6 SERVINGS

Rutabaga Puree

    3 pounds rutabagas, peeled, cut into 1-inch cubes
    3 tablespoons butter

Cook rutabagas in large pot of boiling salted water until very tender, about 45 minutes. Drain well. Transfer to processor; puree until smooth. Return to pot. Stir over medium heat until any excess liquid evaporates. Add butter; stir until melted. Season with salt and pepper. *(Can be made 2 hours ahead. Let stand uncovered at room temperature. Rewarm over medium heat, stirring often.)*

6 SERVINGS

Grilled Asian Pork Chops and Baby Bok Choy

⅓ cup black bean garlic sauce
3 large garlic cloves, minced
1½ tablespoons soy sauce
1½ tablespoons oriental sesame oil
1 tablespoon fresh lime juice
1 tablespoon finely chopped peeled fresh ginger
4 boneless center-cut pork chops (about 8 ounces each)

4 baby bok choy, halved lengthwise

4 lime wedges
2 tablespoons chopped fresh cilantro

Prepare barbecue (medium-high heat). Whisk together black bean sauce, garlic, soy sauce, sesame oil, lime juice, and ginger in shallow dish. Set 2 tablespoons marinade aside. Add pork to remaining marinade; let stand 20 minutes.

Remove pork from marinade; brush cut side of bok choy with reserved 2 tablespoons marinade. Grill pork until just cooked through and thermometer inserted into thickest part registers 145°F, about 5 minutes per side. Grill bok choy until softened and lightly charred, about 5 minutes total.

Divide pork, bok choy, and lime wedges among 4 plates. Sprinkle with cilantro and serve.

4 SERVINGS

Panko-Crusted Mustard Pork Cutlets

¾ cup panko (Japanese breadcrumbs) or fresh breadcrumbs made from crustless French bread
1 tablespoon chopped fresh sage
1 teaspoon grated lemon peel
½ teaspoon freshly ground black pepper
1 large egg
2 tablespoons water
1 tablespoon mayonnaise
1 tablespoon Dijon mustard
2 10- to 12-ounce pork cutlets

3 tablespoons garlic-flavored olive oil
Lemon wedges

Combine first 4 ingredients on plate. Whisk egg and 2 tablespoons water in medium bowl to blend. Whisk mayonnaise and mustard in small bowl. Dredge pork cutlets with mayonnaise-mustard mixture; dip into beaten egg, then coat cutlets with panko crumb mixture. Transfer to plate.

Heat oil in heavy medium skillet over medium-high heat. Add pork; cook until no longer pink on inside and crumbs are golden brown, about 5 minutes per side. Transfer to plates. Serve with lemon wedges.

2 SERVINGS

Panko are fluffy white Japanese breadcrumbs that make a light, crisp crust when fried. Look for them in the Asian foods section of most supermarkets. This dish easily doubles for a dinner party. Serve the chops with steamed spinach and scalloped potatoes.

Baked Baby Back Ribs with Lemon Confit Marinade

    4 large lemons

    8 large garlic cloves, peeled
 ¼ cup olive oil
    3 tablespoons chopped fresh thyme
    3 tablespoons (scant) coarsely chopped fresh rosemary
    2 tablespoons fennel seeds, ground
    2 tablespoons coarse kosher salt
    1 tablespoon freshly ground black pepper
    1 tablespoon (packed) golden brown sugar
    5 pounds meaty baby back pork ribs (about 4 large racks)

In a classic confit, meat cooks (and is then preserved) in its own fat. Here, lemons cook in their own juices to become the basis for an overnight marinade.

Make 4 vertical cuts, about ½ inch deep and 2 inches long, in skin of each lemon. Place lemons in microwave-safe bowl (such as soufflé dish). Cover and cook in microwave on high until skins soften and lemons release juices, about 8 minutes. Uncover and cool lemons 15 minutes. Cut lemons in half. Squeeze juice into strainer set over small bowl; reserve juice. Scoop out and discard lemon pulp and white pith from halves; reserve rinds.

Combine 6 tablespoons reserved lemon juice, lemon rinds, garlic, olive oil, and next 6 ingredients in processor and grind to paste. Generously smear paste on both sides of ribs. Arrange ribs, meaty side up, on 2 large rimmed baking sheets. Cover with plastic; chill overnight.

Position 1 rack in top third and 1 rack in bottom third of oven and preheat to 350°F. Scrape some of marinade off ribs. Place baking sheets with ribs in oven. Bake ribs 30 minutes. Reverse position of baking sheets and roast until ribs are very tender and meat begins to pull away from bones, about 35 minutes longer. Let ribs stand 15 minutes. Transfer to work surface and cut racks between bones into individual ribs. Pile ribs onto platter and serve.

8 SERVINGS

Fig and Rosemary Pork Pot Roast

2 cups dry white wine
1 8-ounce package dried Calimyrna figs, stemmed, halved lengthwise

1 tablespoon olive oil
1 6-rib blade-end or center-cut pork loin roast, chine bone removed, ribs cracked

1 medium onion, chopped
1 medium carrot, peeled, chopped
1 tablespoon chopped fresh rosemary
2 garlic cloves, chopped
1 14-ounce can low-salt chicken broth

1 tablespoon butter, room temperature
1 tablespoon all purpose flour
2 tablespoons Dijon mustard

Preheat oven to 300°F. Bring wine and figs to boil in small saucepan. Remove from heat and let stand until figs soften, about 15 minutes. Drain figs, reserving wine and figs separately.

Meanwhile, heat oil in heavy large ovenproof pot over medium-high heat. Sprinkle pork with salt and pepper. Add to pot and cook until browned on all sides, about 8 minutes total. Transfer to platter.

Add onion and carrot to same pot. Cover and reduce heat to medium-low. Cook until onion is golden brown, stirring occasionally, about 8 minutes. Stir in rosemary and garlic; sauté 1 minute. Add broth and reserved wine.

Return pork to pot, meat side down. Bring to boil. Cover and transfer to oven. Bake until thermometer inserted into center of roast registers 150°F, adding figs during last 10 minutes of roasting, about 1 1/2 hours.

Transfer pork to cutting board. Using slotted spoon, transfer figs to small bowl. Tent pork and figs with foil to keep warm. Spoon fat from surface of sauce. Bring sauce to boil. Stir butter and flour in medium bowl to blend. Whisk 1 cup sauce and mustard into butter mixture. Whisk mustard-butter mixture into sauce in pot. Boil sauce until thickened and slightly reduced, about 8 minutes. Season to taste with salt and pepper.

Transfer pork to platter, surround with figs, and pour sauce over. Carve pork between rib bones.

6 SERVINGS

Bourbon-Molasses Chicken Drumsticks

- ¼ cup (½ stick) butter
- 1 cup minced onion
- 1 cup ketchup
- ¼ cup molasses
- 2 tablespoons (packed) brown sugar
- 1½ tablespoons Worcestershire sauce
- 2 teaspoons yellow mustard
- ¾ teaspoon ground black pepper, divided
- ¼ teaspoon chili powder
- ¼ cup bourbon

- 1½ teaspoons coarse kosher salt
- 12 chicken drumsticks

Melt butter in large saucepan over medium heat. Add onion; sauté until soft, about 6 minutes. Add next 5 ingredients, ¼ teaspoon pepper, and chili powder. Reduce heat to medium-low; simmer until sauce thickens, about 15 minutes. Stir in bourbon; cook until heated through, about 3 minutes. Season with salt. *(Can be made 1 day ahead. Cover and chill.)*

Mix 1½ teaspoons salt and ½ teaspoon pepper in bowl. Loosen skin on drumsticks. Rub salt and pepper mixture under skin without tearing skin. Cover; let stand at room temperature 30 minutes.

Prepare barbecue (medium heat). Grill drumsticks until skin is crisp and juices run clear, turning to cook all sides, about 25 minutes. Transfer ½ cup barbecue sauce to small bowl; reserve. Brush drumsticks with remaining sauce and cook until glaze forms, about 3 minutes longer. Transfer drumsticks to platter and serve with reserved sauce.

4 SERVINGS

POULTRY

Mojito-Marinated Chicken Breasts

¾   cup fresh lime juice

½   cup plus 2 tablespoons light rum

½   cup finely chopped fresh mint

6   tablespoons mint syrup

1   tablespoon vegetable oil

1   tablespoon coarse kosher salt

6   chicken breast halves with skin and bones (about 5 pounds)

3   large limes, quartered lengthwise

    Fresh mint sprigs

The popular rum-and-mint cocktail from Cuba was the inspiration for this entrée. You can find mint syrup on the shelf with the coffee and tea at the supermarket. A last-minute spritz of grilled lime to the chicken adds even more flavor. Garnish with grilled pineapple slices cut into star shapes, if desired.

Whisk lime juice, ½ cup rum, and next 4 ingredients in bowl. Place chicken in resealable plastic bag. Pour marinade over; seal bag. Turn bag to distribute marinade. Chill 4 hours, turning bag twice.

Place lime quarters in shallow bowl. Pour remaining 2 tablespoons rum over, tossing to coat. Let stand at room temperature.

Prepare barbecue (medium heat). Grill chicken until cooked through, about 15 minutes per side. Transfer to platter.

Grill limes until soft and slightly charred, about 5 minutes. Garnish platter with mint sprigs. Squeeze grilled limes over chicken and serve.

6 SERVINGS

Honey-Glazed Lemon Chicken

2 6½- to 7-pound roasting chickens, rinsed, patted dry
2½ cups fresh lemon juice (from about 12 large lemons)

Coarse kosher salt
Freshly ground black pepper

½ cup honey, heated until pourable

Place each chicken in heavy-duty resealable plastic bag. Add 1¼ cups lemon juice to each. Seal bags; turn chickens to coat. Chill at least 6 hours and up to 1 day, turning occasionally.

Preheat oven to 450°F. Drain chickens; pat dry. Sprinkle each with salt and pepper. Place chickens side by side, breast side down, on racks in large roasting pan. Roast 15 minutes. Reduce oven temperature to 375°F. Roast 45 minutes.

Turn chickens breast side up. Brush all over with honey. Continue to roast until cooked through and deep brown, basting with any juices in pan and brushing with honey occasionally, about 55 minutes longer. Transfer to platter. Tent with foil; let stand 15 minutes.

Meanwhile, pour pan juices into small saucepan. Spoon off fat. Rewarm pan juices. Season with salt and pepper. Serve chickens with pan juices.

8 SERVINGS

Herbed Chicken and Arugula Panini

1 pound thin chicken cutlets
1½ tablespoons chopped fresh thyme, divided
6 tablespoons olive oil, divided

2 garlic cloves, finely chopped
3 tablespoons balsamic vinegar

8 ⅓- to ½-inch-thick slices olive bread or 4 crusty sandwich rolls
½ red onion, thinly sliced
1 bunch arugula

Sprinkle chicken on both sides with salt and pepper, then 1 tablespoon thyme. Heat 2 tablespoons olive oil in heavy large skillet over medium-high heat. Add chicken; sauté until golden and cooked through, about 2 minutes per side. Transfer chicken to plate.

Add remaining 4 tablespoons oil and garlic to skillet; stir over medium heat 15 seconds. Add vinegar and remaining ½ tablespoon thyme; cook 15 seconds, scraping up browned bits. Return chicken to skillet and toss until heated through, about 1 minute.

Arrange 1 bread slice on each of 4 plates. Top with chicken, onion, and arugula, then drizzle with vinaigrette from skillet. Top with remaining bread.

4 SERVINGS

Mediterranean Chicken

6 tablespoons olive oil, divided
8 skinless boneless chicken breast halves (about 2½ pounds)

1½ pounds assorted wild mushrooms (such as oyster, crimini, and stemmed shiitake), sliced
1½ cups low-salt chicken broth
⅔ cup pitted Kalamata olives
3 plum tomatoes, seeded, diced
3 garlic cloves, minced
1 tablespoon chopped shallot
1 tablespoon drained capers
2 tablespoons (¼ stick) chilled butter
1 cup teardrop tomatoes (red and yellow)

3 tablespoons chopped fresh parsley
3 tablespoons pine nuts, toasted
Caper berries, halved (optional)

Preheat oven to 200°F. Heat 3 tablespoons oil in large skillet over high heat. Sprinkle chicken with salt and pepper. Working in 2 batches, add chicken to skillet. Cook until brown and just cooked through, about 3 minutes per side. Transfer to ovenproof plate and place in oven to keep warm. Discard oil from skillet.

Add 3 tablespoons oil to same skillet over high heat. Add mushrooms; sauté until wilted and beginning to brown, about 3 minutes. Add broth; boil until almost all liquid evaporates, about 5 minutes. Add olives, plum tomatoes, garlic, shallot, and capers. Sprinkle with salt and pepper. Reduce heat to medium and simmer until liquid is reduced by half, about 7 minutes. Add butter; stir until melted. Mix in teardrop tomatoes. Season to taste with salt and pepper.

Spoon mushroom mixture over chicken. Sprinkle parsley and pine nuts over. Garnish with caper berries, if desired, and serve.

8 SERVINGS

Farmers' Market Dinner for 8

Fava Bean Crostini with Pecorino and Lemon Oil
(page 25)

Mediterranean Chicken
(at left, pictured opposite)

Spinach and Roasted Red Pepper Gratin
(page 144)

Roasted Potatoes

Pinot Grigio

Almond, Apricot, and Cherry Tart
(page 174)

Chicken Breasts with Fennel-Mustard Butter and Radicchio

FENNEL-MUSTARD BUTTER

- 1 tablespoon fennel seeds
- ½ cup (1 stick) butter, room temperature
- 1 tablespoon fresh lemon juice
- 2 teaspoons Dijon mustard
- 1 garlic clove, minced

CHICKEN

- ¼ cup olive oil
- 2 tablespoons fresh lemon juice
- 1 garlic clove, minced
- 6 skinless boneless chicken breast halves, pounded to ⅓-inch thickness
- 4 anchovy fillets, chopped
- 4 cups thinly sliced radicchio
- 2 tablespoons drained capers

FOR FENNEL-MUSTARD BUTTER: Stir fennel seeds in small skillet over high heat until beginning to brown, about 1 minute. Place in spice mill and grind to coarse powder. Transfer to small bowl. Add remaining ingredients; stir to blend. Season with salt and pepper. *(Can be made 2 days ahead. Cover and chill.)*

FOR CHICKEN: Whisk oil, lemon juice, and garlic in small bowl to blend. Place chicken in 13x9x2-inch glass baking dish. Sprinkle with salt and pepper. Pour oil mixture over. Turn to coat. Cover with plastic; chill at least 1 hour and up to 3 hours.

Heat 2 heavy large skillets over medium-high heat. Add 3 chicken breasts with some of marinade to each skillet; sauté until cooked through, about 3 minutes per side. Transfer chicken to platter. Place 2 teaspoons fennel-mustard butter atop each chicken breast. Melt 1/4 cup butter in 1 skillet over medium-high heat. Add anchovies; mash with fork. Stir in radicchio and capers; sauté until radicchio just begins to wilt, about 1 minute. Spoon radicchio atop chicken.

6 SERVINGS

Once the mustard butter is prepared and the chicken is marinated, this quick sauté comes together in just minutes. Any leftover fennel-mustard butter makes an instant sauce dolloped onto grilled fish. Serve with an orzo salad and a crisp Sauvignon Blanc.

Tandoori-Style Chicken

2½ tablespoons paprika
2½ tablespoons turmeric
2½ tablespoons ground cumin
2½ tablespoons garam masala*
 2 tablespoons salt
2½ teaspoons ground cardamom
 2 teaspoons cayenne pepper
 8 large chicken thighs with bones, skin removed
 8 large chicken breast halves with bones, skin removed
 4 cups plain whole-milk yogurt
 2 large onions, coarsely grated

Marinating the chicken in the yogurt mixture overnight tenderizes the meat and adds a delicious tang.

Mix first 7 ingredients in small bowl to blend. Using sharp knife, cut three 3/4-inch-deep diagonal slashes in each chicken piece. Divide chicken between 2 large bowls and rub with spice mixture. Let stand 10 minutes. Divide yogurt and onions between same bowls. Toss chicken to coat. Cover and refrigerate overnight.

Preheat oven to 500°F. Line 2 rimmed baking sheets with foil; place cooling racks on prepared baking sheets. Using slotted spoon, transfer chicken thighs to 1 sheet and chicken breasts to second sheet, spacing pieces slightly apart (make sure that chicken pieces do not touch and are covered in yogurt mixture). Bake until chicken is cooked through, about 30 minutes for breasts and about 40 minutes for thighs. (*Chicken can be made 1 day ahead. Refrigerate until cold, then cover and keep refrigerated.*) Place chicken on large platter. Serve cold or at room temperature.

An Indian spice mixture available in the spice section of many supermarkets and at Indian markets.

8 SERVINGS

Moroccan Chicken with Eggplant, Tomatoes, and Almonds

     6 tablespoons olive oil, divided
     3 cups sliced onions
     6 large garlic cloves, minced
     1 tablespoon Hungarian sweet paprika
  1½ teaspoons coarse kosher salt
     1 teaspoon turmeric
     1 teaspoon ground coriander
     1 teaspoon fennel seeds, ground
     1 teaspoon freshly ground black pepper
    ½ teaspoon ground cumin
    ½ teaspoon ground ginger
     2 cups drained canned diced tomatoes (from 28-ounce can)
     1 cup water
     3 tablespoons (or more) fresh lemon juice
     8 chicken thighs with bones, skinned
     8 chicken drumsticks, skinned

     1 large eggplant, unpeeled, cut into 1-inch cubes

     1 tablespoon chopped fresh marjoram
    ½ cup whole blanched almonds or slivered almonds, toasted
       Chopped fresh cilantro

Heat 2 tablespoons olive oil in heavy large wide pot over medium heat. Add onions and garlic. Cover and cook until onions are soft, about 10 minutes. Add paprika, salt, turmeric, coriander, fennel, pepper, cumin, and ginger; stir 1 minute. Add tomatoes, 1 cup water, and 3 tablespoons lemon juice; bring to boil. Arrange all chicken in single layer in pot; spoon some sauce over. Bring to boil. Reduce heat to medium-low, cover, and simmer 15 minutes. Turn chicken over, cover, and simmer until chicken is tender, about 20 minutes longer.

   Meanwhile, preheat oven to 400°F. Brush large rimmed baking sheet with olive oil. Place eggplant and remaining 4 tablespoons olive oil in large bowl; toss to coat. Spread eggplant out on prepared baking sheet and bake until soft and brown, stirring occasionally, about 25 minutes. *(Chicken and eggplant can be made 1 day ahead. Cool slightly. Refrigerate separately until cold, then cover and keep refrigerated.)*

   Stir eggplant and marjoram into chicken. Simmer uncovered 10 minutes to heat through and blend flavors. Season stew to taste with more lemon juice, if desired, and salt and pepper. Transfer chicken to large shallow bowl. Sprinkle with almonds and cilantro.

8 SERVINGS

Warm Lemon-Cumin Chicken on Pita Bread Salad

4 skinless boneless chicken breast halves
¼ cup plus 6 tablespoons olive oil
2 garlic cloves, minced
6 tablespoons lemon juice, divided
6 teaspoons ground cumin, divided
2 teaspoons grated lemon peel

3 stale pita breads, cut into ¼-inch squares
1 cup chopped fresh Italian parsley or cilantro
6 plum tomatoes, chopped
4 green onions, chopped
½ cup plus 2 tablespoons chopped fresh mint

Using stale pita will keep the bread from getting soggy in the salad.

Combine chicken and ¼ cup oil in large bowl. Add garlic, 3 tablespoons lemon juice, 5 teaspoons cumin, and lemon peel. Rub mixture into chicken to coat. Cover; chill overnight.

Preheat oven to 400°F. Combine remaining 6 tablespoons oil, 3 tablespoons lemon juice, 1 teaspoon cumin, pita bread, parsley, tomatoes, green onions, and ½ cup mint in large bowl. Season salad with salt and pepper. Cover and refrigerate while cooking chicken.

Transfer chicken from marinade to rimmed baking sheet; sprinkle with salt. Bake chicken 10 minutes; turn over and bake until cooked through, about 10 minutes longer. Place chicken on cutting board; slice each breast crosswise into 5 pieces. Arrange salad on large platter. Place chicken atop salad; pour any drippings from baking sheet over chicken. Garnish with remaining 2 tablespoons mint.

6 SERVINGS

Chicken with Garlic and White Wine

2 3½-pound whole chickens, each cut into 8 pieces
5 whole heads of garlic, cloves separated (about 70), unpeeled

6 tablespoons extra-virgin olive oil, divided
2 cups dry white wine
6 very large fresh thyme sprigs

Catalan Spinach (see recipe)

Trim excess fat off chicken. Sprinkle chicken with salt and pepper. Lightly smash garlic cloves just to flatten slightly, leaving peel attached and cloves as whole as possible.

Heat 4 tablespoons olive oil in heavy large pot over medium-high heat. Working in 2 batches, add chicken and cook until brown on all sides, about 12 minutes per batch. Transfer to plate. Add 2 tablespoons oil and garlic to pot. Stir until golden, about 4 minutes. Add wine and thyme; bring to boil. Return chicken to pot. Reduce heat to medium, cover, and simmer until chicken is cooked through, moving chicken pieces from top to bottom every 5 minutes (sauce will not cover chicken), about 20 minutes. Season with salt and pepper.

Transfer chicken to platter. Spoon garlic cloves around chicken and drizzle sauce over. Serve with Catalan Spinach.

8 SERVINGS

Catalan Spinach

6 tablespoons olive oil, divided
2 medium Golden Delicious apples, peeled, cored, cut into ½-inch cubes
1 cup pine nuts
3 shallots, finely chopped
1 cup raisins
3 9-ounce packages fresh spinach

Heat 1 tablespoon oil in each of 2 heavy large pots over high heat. Divide apples between pots and sauté until golden brown around edges, about 3 minutes. Divide pine nuts between pots; sauté until pine nuts are lightly toasted, about 3 minutes. Add 2 tablespoons olive oil to each pot. Divide shallots and raisins between pots; stir to combine. Divide spinach between pots; cover and cook just until wilted, stirring occasionally, about 2 minutes. Season with salt and pepper.

8 SERVINGS

Supper in the Kitchen for 8

Fried Calamari with Rouille, Cherry Peppers, and Lemon
(page 10)

Chicken with Garlic and White Wine
(at left, pictured opposite)

Mashed Potatoes

Chardonnay

Lemon Crème Brûlée Tart
(page 172)

Spicy Turkey Burgers

1¼ pounds lean ground turkey

  1 cup mild salsa, divided

  ½ cup finely chopped shallots

  ¼ cup chopped fresh cilantro

  4 tablespoons vegetable oil, divided

  1 tablespoon chipotle-flavored hot sauce

  1 teaspoon ground cumin

  1 teaspoon salt

  ½ teaspoon ground black pepper

  4 crusty rolls, halved horizontally, toasted if desired

  4 lettuce leaves

Mix ground turkey, ½ cup salsa, shallots, cilantro, 3 tablespoons oil, hot sauce, cumin, salt, and pepper in large bowl. Shape turkey mixture into four 3½- to 4-inch-diameter patties.

Heat 1 tablespoon oil in large nonstick skillet over medium-high heat. Add burgers; cook until brown, about 3 minutes per side. Reduce heat to low. Sauté until burgers are cooked through, about 4 minutes, turning occasionally.

Arrange roll bottoms on 4 plates. Place lettuce, then burgers on roll bottoms. Top each burger with 2 tablespoons of remaining salsa, then roll tops.

4 SERVINGS

Turkey Osso Buco

- 1 teaspoon dried thyme
- 2 whole turkey legs (about 3¼ pounds total), cut at joints into drumsticks and thighs, skin removed
- 1 tablespoon olive oil
- 2 medium onions, chopped
- 2 medium carrots, peeled, chopped
- 2 celery stalks, chopped
- 6 garlic cloves, minced, divided
- ½ cup dry red wine
- 1 28-ounce can diced tomatoes in juice

- ¼ cup chopped fresh Italian parsley
- 1 teaspoon grated lemon peel

Rub thyme over turkey; sprinkle with salt and pepper. Transfer to 6-quart slow cooker. Heat oil in large nonstick skillet over medium-high heat. Add onions, carrots, and celery; sauté 8 minutes. Stir in 4 minced garlic cloves. Transfer vegetables to slow cooker. Add wine to skillet; boil until reduced by ⅓, about 1 minute. Pour wine and tomatoes with juice over turkey. Cover; cook on high until turkey is very tender and falls off bone, about 5½ hours.

Mix parsley, lemon peel, and remaining garlic in bowl for gremolata. Using slotted spoon, remove turkey from pot. Pull meat from bones; divide meat among 6 bowls. Season sauce with salt and pepper; spoon over turkey. Sprinkle with gremolata.

6 SERVINGS

Pool Party for 8

Chips and Guacamole

Raspberry Lemonade
(page 37)

Margaritas and *Beer*

Spicy Turkey Burgers
(double recipe; opposite, pictured opposite)

Mixed Greens with Honey-Lime Dressing
(page 154)

Dilled Potato and Pickled Cucumber Salad
(page 156)

Lemon Sorbet with Mixed Berries

Thyme-Roasted Turkey with Fresh Thyme Gravy

TURKEY

- 1 14-pound turkey; neck, gizzard, and heart reserved
- 3 tablespoons chopped fresh thyme
- ¼ cup (½ stick) unsalted butter, room temperature
- 2 large celery stalks, chopped
- 1 large onion, chopped
- 1 large carrot, chopped

- 4 14-ounce cans low-salt chicken broth

GRAVY

- Low-salt chicken broth

- 1½ tablespoons chopped fresh thyme
- 2 tablespoons all purpose flour
- Pinch of ground allspice

FOR TURKEY: Rinse turkey inside and out; pat dry. Starting at neck end, slide hand between skin and breast meat to loosen skin. Spread 3 tablespoons thyme over breast meat under skin. Tuck wings under. Tie legs loosely together. Sprinkle turkey all over with salt and pepper. Smear turkey with butter. Place on rack set in large roasting pan. Add turkey neck, gizzard, heart, chopped celery, onion, and carrot to pan. (*Can be prepared 1 day ahead. Cover and refrigerate.*)

Set rack at lowest position in oven and preheat to 375°F. Pour 1 can broth into pan around turkey. Roast turkey 30 minutes. Reduce oven temperature to 350°F. Turn pan around. Roast turkey 30 minutes. Pour 1 can broth over turkey. Roast 30 minutes. Pour 1 can broth over turkey. Roast 30 minutes. Pour remaining can of broth over turkey. Turn pan around. Roast turkey until thermometer inserted into thickest part of thigh registers 175°F, covering turkey loosely with aluminum foil if browning too quickly, about 30 minutes longer. Transfer turkey to platter; let rest 30 to 40 minutes (internal temperature will increase 5 to 10 degrees).

FOR GRAVY: Strain pan juices into large glass measuring cup. Spoon 2 tablespoons fat from surface into heavy medium saucepan. Spoon off and discard remaining fat from pan juices. If necessary, add enough broth to measure 3 cups pan-juice mixture.

Heat fat in saucepan over medium heat. Add thyme and sauté until fragrant, about 1 minute. Add flour and allspice; whisk 1 minute. Gradually whisk in 3 cups pan-juice mixture. Simmer until gravy thickens slightly, about 5 minutes. Season with salt and pepper.

8 SERVINGS

Turkey Piccata with Tarragon Cream

1½ ounces pancetta (Italian bacon) or bacon, cut into ⅓-inch-wide strips

1 cup whipping cream
⅓ cup chopped onion
4 large sprigs fresh tarragon plus 4 teaspoons chopped fresh tarragon
2 teaspoons Dijon mustard

2 12-ounce skinless boneless turkey breast tenderloins
1 tablespoon vegetable oil

Cook pancetta in medium skillet over high heat until crisp, about 2 minutes.

Bring cream, onion, and tarragon sprigs to boil in heavy small saucepan. Remove from heat. Cover and steep 25 minutes. Strain mixture into saucepan. Boil tarragon cream until reduced to ¼ cup, about 4 minutes. Whisk in chopped tarragon and mustard. Season with salt and pepper. Keep warm.

Cut each tenderloin crosswise into 4 pieces. Using mallet, pound each piece between sheets of plastic to ¼-inch thickness. Sprinkle with salt and pepper. Heat oil in large skillet over medium heat. Add turkey and sauté until cooked through, about 2 minutes per side. Transfer turkey to 4 plates. Spoon tarragon cream over and sprinkle with pancetta.

4 SERVINGS

Duck Breast with Crème Fraîche and Roasted Grapes

6 6- to 8-ounce duck breasts (thawed if frozen)
1 tablespoon dried juniper berries, crushed in resealable plastic bag using flat side of mallet*
1 tablespoon fresh thyme leaves

½ pound purple seedless grapes, cut into small clusters
½ tablespoon olive oil
   Coarse kosher salt

3 cups arugula
¼ cup crème fraîche or sour cream, stirred to loosen

Using sharp knife, score skin of duck breast diagonally to create ¾-inch-wide diamond pattern. Sprinkle crushed juniper berries and thyme over both sides of breast; press to adhere. Place on rimmed baking sheet, cover with plastic wrap, and refrigerate at least 4 hours. *(Can be prepared 1 day ahead. Keep refrigerated.)*

Preheat oven to 500°F. Arrange grape clusters in single layer on baking sheet. Drizzle with olive oil and sprinkle with kosher salt and pepper. Roast until skins are slightly crisp but grapes are still soft and juicy inside, about 14 minutes. Cool. (*Can be made 4 hours ahead. Let stand at room temperature.*)

Sprinkle both sides of duck breasts with salt and pepper. Heat heavy large skillet over medium heat. Add duck, skin side down; cook until almost all fat is rendered, about 7 minutes. Increase heat to medium-high and cook until skin is brown and crisp, about 4 minutes. Turn duck over and cook about 3 minutes longer for medium-rare. Let duck rest 5 minutes.

Divide arugula among 6 plates. Thinly slice duck breasts crosswise and fan out slightly; place 1 breast atop arugula on each plate. Drizzle crème fraîche over each breast. Divide grapes among plates.

Juniper berries are available in the spice section of most supermarkets.

6 SERVINGS

Greek-Spiced Game Hen with Clementines, Artichokes, and Olives

1   Cornish game hen (about 1½ pounds), halved
2   teaspoons Greek spice blend

2   small clementines
1   6-ounce jar marinated artichoke hearts
¼   cup pitted assorted Mediterranean olives

¼   cup dry white wine

Preheat oven to 450°F. Sprinkle game hen with salt and pepper. Using fingers, loosen skin and rub spice blend between meat and skin.

Slice unpeeled clementines crosswise. Arrange clementines, artichoke hearts with juices from jar, and olives in single layer in 13x9-inch metal baking pan. Place hen atop clementine mixture.

Roast hen until golden and cooked through, about 25 minutes. Brush with pan juices. Transfer 1 hen half to each of 2 plates. Place baking pan atop burner over medium-high heat. Spoon off excess fat. Add wine to clementine mixture in baking pan. Cook until liquid is reduced to ¼ cup, about 2 minutes. Spoon sauce over hen halves. Spoon clementine mixture alongside and serve.

2 SERVINGS

Midweek Dinner with Friends for 4

Antipasto Platter

Turkey Piccata with Tarragon Cream
(*opposite*)

Green Beans

Rice

Sauvignon Blanc

Pears Poached in Earl Grey Tea with Dried Fruit
(*page 188*)

Seared Tuna Steaks with Spicy Green Onion Mayonnaise

- ½ cup mayonnaise
- 2 tablespoons minced green onions (white and green parts)
- 1 teaspoon (or more) wasabi paste*

- 2 tablespoons teriyaki sauce
- 1 tablespoon soy sauce
- 1 tablespoon unseasoned rice vinegar
- 4 8-ounce tuna steaks (preferably ahi; each about 1 inch thick)

  Vegetable oil

Whisk first 3 ingredients in small bowl to blend, adding more wasabi if desired. Cover; chill.

Whisk teriyaki sauce, soy sauce, and rice vinegar in small bowl to blend. Place tuna steaks in resealable plastic bag. Add teriyaki mixture; seal bag. Turn bag to coat. Let stand at room temperature 30 minutes, turning bag occasionally.

Brush grill with oil. Prepare barbecue (medium-high heat). Drain tuna steaks. Grill tuna to desired doneness, about 4 minutes per side for medium. Serve with spicy mayonnaise.

*Available in tubes in the Asian foods section of some supermarkets and at Japanese markets.

4 SERVINGS

SEAFOOD

Fillet of Cod with Asparagus
and Prosciutto

1½ pounds slender asparagus spears, trimmed to 7-inch lengths

2 garlic cloves, minced

1 teaspoon salt

2 tablespoons (¼ stick) butter

1 tablespoon plus 6 teaspoons olive oil

⅓ cup fresh lemon juice

1½ teaspoons grated lemon peel

½ teaspoon ground black pepper

6 6-ounce cod fillets, pinbones removed

6 ounces paper-thin prosciutto slices, halved lengthwise

Cook asparagus in large pot of boiling salted water until crisp-tender, about 3 minutes. Drain. Transfer to bowl of ice water to cool. Drain.

Mash garlic and 1 teaspoon salt to paste in small bowl. Melt butter with 1 tablespoon oil in small nonstick skillet over medium heat. Add garlic paste; stir until pale golden, about 1 minute. Stir in lemon juice, peel, and ½ teaspoon black pepper. Remove from heat.

Preheat oven to 500°F. Cut out six 12-inch squares of parchment paper. Place 1 parchment square on work surface. Drizzle 1 teaspoon oil over parchment. Place 1 cod fillet in center of parchment. Spoon ⅙ of garlic-lemon mixture over fish. Cover with ⅙ of asparagus spears. Arrange ⅙ of prosciutto slices over. Fold 2 opposite sides of parchment in over fish and vegetables, then fold in remaining 2 sides, enclosing completely. Fasten parchment edges together with paper clips to seal packet. Place on large rimmed baking sheet. Repeat procedure with remaining parchment, oil, fish, garlic-lemon mixture, asparagus, and prosciutto. (*Can be prepared 6 hours ahead. Refrigerate.*)

Bake fish until just opaque in center (parchment will turn golden brown), about 12 minutes. Transfer 1 parchment packet to each of 6 plates. Open parchment packets and serve.

6 SERVINGS

Each serving is baked *en papillote*, or wrapped individually in parchment paper to lock in steam for a more succulent result.

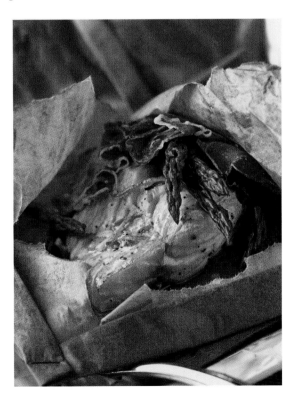

Salmon with Sesame and Orange-Ginger Relish

⅓ cup dry white wine
⅓ cup fresh orange juice
2½ tablespoons soy sauce
1 2½-pound salmon fillet

3 large navel oranges

½ cup matchstick-size strips red pepper
½ cup thinly sliced red onion
2½ tablespoons chopped fresh cilantro
2 teaspoons minced peeled fresh ginger
2 teaspoons grated orange peel
1 teaspoon oriental sesame oil
½ teaspoon coarse kosher salt
¼ teaspoon dried crushed red pepper

Vegetable oil
1 tablespoon sesame seeds, toasted

Whisk first 3 ingredients in small bowl to blend; transfer to 13x9x2-inch glass baking dish. Place salmon, skin side up, in orange juice mixture; cover with plastic and chill at least 2 hours and up to 4 hours. Bring to room temperature 30 minutes before cooking.

Using small sharp knife, cut peel and white pith from oranges. Working over bowl, cut between membranes to release segments into bowl.

Mix red pepper and next 7 ingredients in medium bowl to blend. Fold in reserved orange segments and any accumulated juices. (*Can be prepared 1 hour ahead. Let stand at room temperature.*)

Preheat oven to 450°F. Line rimmed baking sheet with foil; generously brush with vegetable oil. Place fish, skin side down, on prepared baking sheet. Sprinkle with salt and pepper. Bake until fish is just opaque in center, about 20 minutes. Using large spatula, gently loosen salmon from foil. Using foil as aid, carefully lift salmon from sheet and allow salmon to slide from foil onto platter. Mound orange relish down center of fish, sprinkle with sesame seeds, and serve.

8 SERVINGS

Halibut with Capers, Tomatoes, and Olives

    4 6- to 7-ounce halibut fillets
       All purpose flour
    4 tablespoons olive oil, divided
    2 large shallots, chopped
  ¼ teaspoon dried crushed red pepper
    4 plum tomatoes, seeded, chopped
  ½ cup chopped pitted Kalamata olives
  ½ cup chopped fresh basil, divided
    1 tablespoon drained capers
  ⅓ cup bottled clam juice
  ¼ cup dry white wine

Sprinkle fish with salt and pepper. Dredge in flour. Heat 2 tablespoons oil in heavy large skillet over medium-high heat. Add fish and sauté until lightly browned and just opaque in center, about 4 minutes per side. Transfer fish to platter. Heat remaining 2 tablespoons oil in same skillet. Add shallots and crushed red pepper; sauté 1 minute. Mix in tomatoes, olives, ¼ cup basil, and capers. Add clam juice and wine. Boil until sauce thickens slightly, about 4 minutes. Mix in ¼ cup basil. Season with salt and pepper. Spoon over fish.

4 SERVINGS

Grilled Mahi-Mahi with Avocado-Melon Salsa

- 1 small avocado, diced
- 1 cup 1/3-inch cubes cantaloupe
- 1/2 cup diced red onion
- 1/3 cup chopped fresh cilantro
- 3 tablespoons fresh lime juice
- 3/4 teaspoon grated lime peel

- 4 6-ounce mahi-mahi fillets (each about 1 inch thick)
- 1 tablespoon olive oil
- 3 tablespoons Jamaican jerk seasoning

Jamaican jerk seasoning—a blend of chiles, thyme, garlic, onion, and spices—gives the grilled fish a reddish-brown finish. It's a supermarket staple now; look for it in the spice aisle. Serve this with rice salad and grilled squash.

Oil grill rack. Prepare barbecue (medium-high heat). Toss first 6 ingredients in medium bowl to blend. Season salsa generously with salt and pepper. Set aside.

Brush fish with 1 tablespoon oil. Spread seasoning in dish. Dredge fish in seasoning, turning to coat. Grill fish until just opaque in center, about 4 minutes per side. Serve with salsa.

4 SERVINGS

Broiled Swordfish à la Niçoise

12 cups water

1¼ cups pearl barley

½ pound haricots verts, trimmed

2 cups grape tomatoes, halved

1 cup pitted Kalamata olives, halved

1 medium-size red onion, sliced

⅓ cup plus ½ cup olive oil

3 tablespoons fresh lemon juice

1 tablespoon chopped fresh thyme

1 teaspoon grated lemon peel

3 garlic cloves, minced

8 6-ounce swordfish steaks

2 medium-size red bell peppers, thinly sliced

2 medium-size yellow bell peppers, thinly sliced

Lemon wedges

Bring 12 cups water to boil in large pot. Add barley. Cover pot; reduce heat to medium. Simmer until barley is tender, about 30 minutes. Add haricots verts; boil until tender, about 5 minutes. Drain. Place mixture in large bowl. Mix in tomatoes, olives, onion, 1/3 cup oil, lemon juice, thyme, and lemon peel. *(Barley can be made 2 hours ahead. Cover and let stand at room temperature.)*

Preheat broiler. Whisk 1/2 cup oil and garlic in bowl. Turn fish in oil mixture; divide fish between 2 rimmed baking sheets. Toss peppers in oil mixture; divide between baking sheets. Drizzle remaining oil from bowl over fish and peppers. Sprinkle with salt and pepper.

Place 1 pan in broiler 3 minutes. Turn fish over; broil until fish is opaque in center and peppers begin to blacken, about 2 minutes longer. Repeat with remaining fish and peppers. Divide barley salad among plates. Top with fish and peppers and drizzle with pan juices. Serve with lemon wedges.

8 SERVINGS

Fish Skewers with Tarragon Vinaigrette

- 1/3 cup olive oil
- 1/4 cup white wine vinegar
- 2 tablespoons minced shallots
- 1 tablespoon chopped fresh tarragon
- 1 tablespoon Dijon mustard
- 1 pound tuna, monkfish, or halibut fillets, cut into 1-inch chunks

- 6 cups mixed baby greens

Shrimp or sea scallops would also work well in this recipe. Team the skewers with grilled plum tomatoes, herbed orzo salad, and grilled French bread for a terrific supper.

Prepare barbecue (medium-high heat). Whisk olive oil, white wine vinegar, minced shallots, tarragon, and Dijon mustard in small bowl to blend. Season vinaigrette to taste with salt and pepper. Place fish in pie dish. Pour half of vinaigrette over and turn to coat. Marinate 15 minutes at room temperature.

Thread fish onto 4 metal skewers, about 5 fish chunks per skewer. Grill until fish chunks are just opaque in center, turning occasionally, about 5 minutes.

Meanwhile, toss baby greens with remaining tarragon vinaigrette. Divide salad among 4 plates. Place fish skewers atop greens and serve.

4 SERVINGS

Red Snapper Baked in Salt with Romesco Sauce

SAUCE

- 3 large plum tomatoes
- 2 large red bell peppers
- 1 medium onion (unpeeled)
- 4 tablespoons olive oil, divided

- 1 dried ancho chile*

- ½ cup sliced almonds
- ¼ cup extra-virgin olive oil
- 3 garlic cloves
- 2 tablespoons Sherry wine vinegar
- 1 slice wheat bread, toasted, cut into ½-inch cubes (about ½ cup)
- 1 teaspoon imported sweet paprika

FISH

- 2 2-pound whole red snappers
- 6 pounds coarse kosher salt
- 3 cups water

FOR SAUCE: Preheat oven to 400°F. Toss tomatoes, bell peppers, and onion in small baking dish with 2 tablespoons olive oil. Roast until partially charred, turning every 15 minutes, about 45 minutes. Cover with foil; let stand 15 minutes.

Meanwhile, heat 1 tablespoon olive oil in small skillet over medium-high heat. Add chile; fry until darkened and slightly puffed, turning once, about 30 seconds. Transfer to small bowl. Add enough hot water to cover. Let stand 30 minutes.

Peel and seed ancho chile, tomatoes, and bell peppers; place in blender. Peel onion; coarsely chop and add to blender.

Heat 1 tablespoon olive oil in small skillet over medium-high heat. Add almonds; sauté until lightly toasted, about 1 minute. Transfer to blender. Add ¼ cup extra-virgin olive oil, garlic, vinegar, bread, and paprika to blender; blend to coarse puree. Transfer to bowl; season with salt. (*Can be made 1 day ahead. Cover and chill. Bring to room temperature before serving.*)

FOR FISH: Preheat oven to 450°F. Place 1 fish in each of two 13x9x2-inch metal baking pans. Cover each fish with 3 pounds salt. Drizzle 1½ cups water over salt in each pan. Using hands, pack salt over fish to cover completely.

Bake fish until thermometer inserted into center of fish registers 135°F, about 30 minutes. Gently rap salt crust with back of spoon to crack; carefully remove salt. Use pastry brush to remove any remaining salt. Carefully transfer whole fish to platter and serve with sauce.

Ancho chiles are available in some supermarkets, Latin American markets, and specialty foods stores.

4 SERVINGS

The salt creates a seal around the fish, which preserves its moisture and pure flavors. Romesco is a classic sauce from the Catalonia region of Spain. For cooking the fish, use two 13x9x2-inch metal baking pans.

Grouper Sandwiches with Wasabi Coleslaw

- 2 cups thinly sliced red cabbage
- ¼ cup wasabi mayonnaise*
- 2 tablespoons rice vinegar
- 4 5-ounce grouper fillets or other firm white fish
- ½ cup panko (Japanese breadcrumbs)* or fresh breadcrumbs made from crustless French bread
- 3 tablespoons vegetable oil
- 4 sesame-seed sandwich buns, split

   Lemon wedges

To make things even easier, use a cabbage slaw mix.

Stir together cabbage, wasabi mayonnaise, and vinegar in medium bowl. Let stand 15 minutes. Sprinkle fish fillets on both sides with salt and pepper. Place panko in shallow dish. Dredge fish in panko, turning to coat evenly.

Heat oil in heavy large nonstick skillet over medium-high heat. Add fish fillets and cook until golden brown and opaque in center, about 4 minutes per side.

Meanwhile, toast sandwich buns.

Place 1 bun bottom on each of 4 plates. Top each with fish. Squeeze lemon over fish. Spoon slaw over. Cover with bun tops and serve.

Sold in the Asian foods section of some supermarkets and in Asian markets.

MAKES 4

Spicy Red Fish Stew

    3 large red bell peppers
    5 tablespoons extra-virgin olive oil
   12 shallots, chopped
    2 14½-ounce cans chopped tomatoes in juice
    2 garlic cloves, minced
   ¾ teaspoon dried crushed red pepper
   ½ cup chopped fresh cilantro
    1 teaspoon grated lemon peel
    2 pounds halibut or cod fillets, cut into 1-inch pieces

Char bell peppers over flame or in broiler until blackened on all sides. Enclose peppers in paper bag 10 minutes. Peel, seed, and chop peppers. Heat oil in heavy large skillet over medium heat. Add shallots and sauté until very soft, about 6 minutes. Stir in peppers, tomatoes with juice, garlic, and crushed red pepper. Simmer 10 minutes to blend flavors. Stir in cilantro and lemon peel. Add fish; simmer until just opaque in center, about 5 minutes. Season stew to taste with salt and pepper. Spoon into bowls and serve.

6 SERVINGS

Roasted Tuna with Grapefruit and Tarragon

    1 white grapefruit

    2 tablespoons minced shallots
    2 teaspoons chopped fresh tarragon
   ¼ cup extra-virgin olive oil
    6 6-ounce tuna steaks

Preheat oven to 475°F. Grate 1 teaspoon grapefruit peel; reserve. Cut off peel and pith from grapefruit; cut fruit into six ¼-inch-thick slices and discard seeds.

   Mix shallots, tarragon, and grated grapefruit peel in small bowl to blend. Drizzle olive oil over bottom of medium roasting pan; heat pan in oven 3 minutes. Sprinkle shallot mixture over oil. Place tuna steaks in single layer atop shallot mixture; sprinkle with salt and pepper. Roast 5 minutes. Turn tuna steaks over. Top each with 1 slice grapefruit. Roast tuna to desired doneness, about 5 minutes longer for medium.

6 SERVINGS

Curry-Ginger Fish with Cucumber Relish

½ cup plain nonfat yogurt

4 teaspoons minced peeled fresh ginger, divided

2 garlic cloves, minced

1 teaspoon curry powder

1 teaspoon ground cumin

⅛ teaspoon cayenne pepper

4 5- to 6-ounce halibut steaks or mahi-mahi fillets (each about ¾ to 1 inch thick)

1½ cups diced English hothouse cucumber

2 tablespoons seasoned rice vinegar*

2 tablespoons chopped fresh cilantro

Olive oil
Fresh cilantro sprigs

Start marinating the fish at least four hours ahead so that the spice flavor comes through.

Whisk yogurt, 2 teaspoons minced fresh ginger, garlic, curry powder, cumin, and cayenne pepper in medium bowl to blend. Add fish and turn to coat evenly. Cover and refrigerate at least 4 hours or overnight, turning fish occasionally.

Mix cucumber, vinegar, chopped cilantro, and remaining 2 teaspoons ginger in small bowl. Season lightly to taste with pepper. *(Relish can be made 4 hours ahead. Cover and refrigerate, stirring occasionally.)*

Prepare barbecue (medium-high heat). Brush grill rack with olive oil. Scrape off excess yogurt marinade from fish; sprinkle fish with salt and pepper. Grill fish until just opaque in center, about 6 minutes per side. Transfer fish to plates. Spoon cucumber relish alongside; garnish with cilantro sprigs.

Also known as sushi vinegar; available in the Asian foods section of most supermarkets and at Asian markets.

4 SERVINGS

Scallops and Haricots Verts with Creamy Bacon Vinaigrette

- 6 slices thick-cut bacon, cut crosswise into ½-inch strips
- 12 ounces haricots verts, trimmed, cut crosswise into 1½-inch pieces
- 2 pounds sea scallops, side muscles removed
- ¾ cup white wine vinegar
- ¾ cup water
- 2¼ teaspoons Dijon mustard
- 6 tablespoons whipping cream
- 4 teaspoons chopped fresh dill

Sauté bacon strips in heavy large skillet over medium heat until brown and crisp. Using slotted spoon, transfer bacon to paper towels to drain. Reserve skillet and drippings.

Cook beans in large pot of boiling salted water until crisp-tender, about 5 minutes. Drain; transfer to bowl. Cover loosely with foil.

Heat drippings in reserved skillet over medium heat. Sprinkle scallops with salt and pepper. Working in batches, add scallops to skillet; cook until browned, about 2 minutes per side. Transfer to bowl with beans; cover loosely with foil. Reserve skillet.

Whisk vinegar, water, and mustard into drippings in reserved skillet. Boil over high heat until reduced by half, stirring frequently and scraping up browned bits, about 7 minutes. Stir in whipping cream; bring sauce to boil. Season to taste with salt and pepper.

Add bacon to bowl with beans and scallops; mix gently. Divide mixture among 6 plates. Drizzle with sauce, sprinkle with dill, and serve.

6 SERVINGS

Lunch on the Lawn for 6

Summer Minestrone with Pesto
(page 33)

Scallops and Haricots Verts with Creamy Bacon Vinaigrette
(at left, pictured opposite)

French Bread

Chablis and *Sparkling Water*

Grapefruit, Ginger, and Star Anise Compote
(page 188)

Bay Scallops with Polenta, Wild Mushrooms, Sherry, and Parsley Breadcrumbs

  1 cup fresh breadcrumbs from French bread with crust
  2 tablespoons extra-virgin olive oil
  2 tablespoons chopped fresh parsley

  9 tablespoons unsalted butter, divided
12 ounces fresh chanterelle mushrooms or other fresh wild mushrooms (such as oyster, stemmed shiitake, or crimini, quartered if large)
2½ teaspoons chopped fresh thyme
  1 cup chopped green onions
  ½ cup amontillado Sherry
  ¼ cup low-salt chicken broth
  ¼ cup whipping cream

  4 cups (or more) water
  1 teaspoon salt
  1 cup polenta

  1 pound bay scallops

Preheat oven to 350°F. Toss breadcrumbs with olive oil and parsley in medium bowl to blend. Spread onto rimmed baking sheet. Bake until golden and crunchy, stirring occasionally, about 15 minutes. (*Can be made 1 day ahead. Cool completely. Store in airtight container at room temperature.*)

Melt 4 tablespoons butter in heavy large skillet over medium-high heat. Add mushrooms and thyme. Sauté until mushrooms are tender, stirring occasionally, about 7 minutes. Add green onions; sauté 1 minute. Add Sherry; boil until slightly reduced, about 2 minutes. Add broth. Boil until reduced by half, about 3 minutes. Add cream; simmer until thickened, about 3 minutes. (*Can be made 3 hours ahead. Cover and refrigerate.*)

Bring 4 cups water and 1 teaspoon salt to boil in heavy medium saucepan. Gradually whisk in polenta. Reduce heat to medium-low. Cook polenta until tender, adding more water as needed if too thick, and whisking frequently, about 20 minutes. Stir in 3 tablespoons butter. Season with salt and pepper. Cover to keep warm.

Reheat mushroom mixture. Melt 2 tablespoons butter in another large skillet over high heat. Add scallops and sauté until just translucent in center, about 1 minute. Stir scallops and juices into mushrooms. Season with salt and pepper.

Divide polenta among plates. Spoon scallop mixture over polenta, sprinkle breadcrumbs over, and serve.

2 SERVINGS

Be sure to use a good amontillado, the medium-dry Sherry that is lightly aged to give it a mellow, nutty flavor. Uncork a Condrieu, an aromatic Rhône white made with Viognier grapes to go with the scallops.

Portuguese Clams with Linguiça and Tomatoes

    3 tablespoons olive oil
    8 ounces linguiça, chorizo, or kielbasa sausage, sliced
    1 large onion, chopped
    2 14½-ounce cans diced tomatoes with green pepper and garlic or
       Italian-recipe tomatoes
    4 dozen littleneck or other small hard-shell clams
    1 cup white wine
    ½ teaspoon (or more) hot pepper sauce
    ¼ cup chopped fresh cilantro, divided

Heat oil in Dutch oven over medium-high heat. Add sausage and onion and cook until golden, stirring often, about 5 minutes. Stir in tomatoes with juice, then clams. Pour wine over. Bring to simmer. Cover pan and simmer until clams open, 5 to 10 minutes depending on size of clams (discard any that do not open). Transfer clams to shallow bowls. Bring broth to boil. Season with hot sauce and half of cilantro.

Ladle broth and sausage over clams. Sprinkle with remaining cilantro.

6 SERVINGS

Use the smallest clams you can find. Mussels would also work nicely in this dish. Accompany with crusty French bread and a green salad.

Thai Shrimp Curry

1 tablespoon peanut oil
1 cup thinly sliced onion
1 cup chopped green onions (about 8 small)
1 to 2 tablespoons Thai green curry paste*
1 14-ounce can unsweetened coconut milk*
1 cup low-salt chicken broth
3 tablespoons Thai fish sauce (nam pla)*
2 teaspoons sugar
1 cup diced plum tomatoes
2 pounds uncooked large shrimp, peeled, deveined
   Chopped fresh cilantro
   Lime wedges

Heat peanut oil in heavy large skillet over medium-high heat. Add sliced onion; stir-fry until soft and beginning to brown, about 4 minutes. Reduce heat to medium. Add chopped green onions and curry paste; stir until fragrant, about 1 minute. Add coconut milk, chicken broth, fish sauce, and sugar; bring to boil. Add tomatoes and boil 2 minutes. Add shrimp and cook just until opaque in center, stirring often, about 3 minutes. Transfer curry to large shallow bowl. Garnish with cilantro. Serve, passing lime wedges separately.

Sold in the Asian foods section of some supermarkets and at Asian markets.

8 SERVINGS

This dish bursts with flavor yet is so simple to prepare. Adjust the heat by adding the curry paste to taste.

Garlic-Roasted Shrimp with Red Peppers and Smoked Paprika

   Nonstick vegetable oil spray
3 pounds uncooked jumbo shrimp, peeled with tails left intact, deveined
3 red bell peppers, cut into 1½-inch triangles
6 tablespoons olive oil
6 garlic cloves, minced
2½ tablespoons smoked paprika*
1 teaspoon cayenne pepper

1½ tablespoons chopped fresh oregano
½ cup dry Sherry

Make the preparation of this recipe even easier: Buy frozen peeled deveined shrimp and thaw before cooking.

Spray two 13x9x2-inch metal baking pans with nonstick spray. Mix shrimp, peppers, oil, garlic, smoked paprika, and cayenne in large bowl to coat. Divide mixture between prepared pans, arranging shrimp in single layer. Sprinkle with salt and pepper. (*Can be prepared 8 hours ahead. Cover and chill.*)

Preheat oven to 400°F. Roast shrimp 10 minutes. Turn shrimp; sprinkle with oregano. Roast until shrimp are just opaque in center, about 7 minutes longer. Transfer shrimp and peppers to platter. Place pans over 2 burners on medium heat. Add half of Sherry to each; boil until reduced by half, scraping up browned bits, about 2 minutes. Drizzle over shrimp and serve warm or at room temperature.

Smoked paprika is available in some supermarkets and at Middle Eastern markets and specialty foods stores.

6 SERVINGS

Spanish Noodle Paella

2 cups (about) water, divided
¼ teaspoon saffron threads, crumbled
2 tablespoons olive oil
1 medium onion, finely chopped
1 red bell pepper, finely chopped
4 tablespoons chopped fresh Italian parsley, divided
2 large garlic cloves, chopped
1 pound tomatoes, seeded, chopped
1 tablespoon tomato paste
1 teaspoon Hungarian sweet paprika

3 8-ounce bottles clam juice
1 1¼-pound live lobster

10 ounces spaghetti, broken into 1-inch pieces (about 2⅓ cups)
12 mussels, scrubbed, debearded
12 uncooked large shrimp, peeled, deveined
12 sea scallops, side muscles trimmed

Place 1 tablespoon water in cup; mix in saffron. Heat oil in large saucepan over medium heat. Add onion, bell pepper, 3 tablespoons parsley, and garlic. Sauté until onion is lightly browned, about 4 minutes. Mix in tomatoes. Simmer until almost all tomato juices have evaporated, about 3 minutes. Stir in tomato paste, paprika, and saffron mixture. (*Sauce base can be made 1 day ahead. Cover and chill.*)

Bring clam juice to boil in large wide pot over medium-high heat. Add lobster. Cover;

boil until lobster is red, about 4 minutes. Remove pot from heat. Using tongs, transfer lobster to rimmed baking sheet; reserve lobster broth in pot. Cool lobster 15 minutes. Twist tail off body. Cut tail in half lengthwise; remove meat. Twist off claws. Split claw shells with cleaver and remove meat. Cut meat into 1- to 1½-inch pieces. Strain juices from sheet into 4-cup measuring cup. Strain in broth from pot. If necessary, add enough water to measure 3 cups broth mixture.

Heat sauce base in paella pan or very large skillet over medium heat. Add noodle pieces; stir 1 minute. Add 3 cups broth mixture; bring to boil, stirring occasionally. Reduce heat and simmer until noodles are almost tender, about 12 minutes. Mix in mussels and 1 cup water. Cover and cook until mussels open, about 5 minutes; discard any that do not open. Mix in shrimp, scallops, and lobster. Cover; simmer until seafood is just cooked through, adding water by ¼ cupfuls if paella is dry, about 6 minutes. Uncover; simmer until noodles are tender, about 3 minutes. Season with salt and pepper; sprinkle with 1 tablespoon parsley.

4 TO 6 SERVINGS

Seared Peppered Scallops with Orange-Soy Glaze

4	tablespoons peanut oil, divided
1½	pounds sea scallops, patted dry with paper towels
2	teaspoons ground peppercorn blend, or ground black pepper
2	garlic cloves, finely chopped (about 2 teaspoons)
½	cup orange juice
1	tablespoon soy sauce
½	teaspoon (packed) grated orange peel

To save even more time, buy the peppercorn medley packaged in a pepper grinder in the spice section of the supermarket. Round out the meal with curried rice and sautéed snow peas.

Heat 3 tablespoons oil in large skillet over high heat. Sprinkle scallops with pepper blend and salt. Working in batches, add scallops to skillet in single layer; sauté until brown on outside and just opaque in center, about 2 minutes per side. Transfer scallops to plate, leaving drippings in pan.

Add garlic and remaining 1 tablespoon oil to drippings in skillet; stir 30 seconds. Add orange juice, soy sauce, and orange peel. Boil until sauce thickens to syrup, stirring frequently, about 2 minutes.

Pour sauce over scallops and serve.

4 SERVINGS

Zucchini, Sun-Dried Tomato, and Mozzarella Tart

1 sheet frozen puff pastry (half of 17.3-ounce package), thawed

1½ cups shredded mozzarella cheese

6 tablespoons plus ¼ cup freshly grated Parmesan cheese

½ cup drained oil-packed sun-dried tomatoes, thinly sliced

½ cup thinly sliced fresh basil

¼ cup chopped green onions

1 tablespoon chopped fresh oregano

1 small zucchini, cut into thin rounds

2 large eggs

1 cup half and half

¼ teaspoon salt

¼ teaspoon ground black pepper

Roll out pastry on floured surface to ⅛-inch-thick square. Trim pastry edges to form 13-inch round. Transfer to 11-inch tart pan with removable bottom. Fold in overhang to form double-thick sides. Pierce with fork. Cover; chill 1 hour.

Preheat oven to 425°F. Line pastry with foil; fill with beans or pie weights. Bake pastry until sides are set, about 20 minutes. Remove foil and beans. Bake crust until bottom is

golden brown, pressing with back of fork if bubbles form, about 8 minutes. Cool 5 minutes.

Reduce oven temperature to 400°F. Sprinkle mozzarella over bottom of crust. Top with 6 tablespoons Parmesan, tomatoes, basil, green onions, and oregano. Arrange zucchini rounds in concentric circles to cover top of tart. Whisk eggs, half and half, salt, and pepper in medium bowl. Pour mixture into tart. Sprinkle with remaining 1/4 cup Parmesan.

Bake tart until custard is set and crust is golden brown, about 35 minutes. Serve warm or at room temperature.

6 SERVINGS

Cannellini and Kale Ragout

- 6 tablespoons extra-virgin olive oil, divided
- 4 1½-inch-thick slices Italian bread, crusts removed, each slice quartered
- 1 teaspoon plus 1 tablespoon chopped fresh thyme

- 3 garlic cloves, finely chopped
- ¼ teaspoon dried crushed red pepper
- 5 cups (packed) thinly sliced kale (about 1 large bunch)
- 1 14½-ounce can vegetable broth
- 1 14½-ounce can diced tomatoes with green pepper and onion in juice
- 1 15-ounce can cannellini (white kidney beans), drained

The oversize croutons add a nice crunch to this warming dish, which is a cross between a soup and a stew. Romaine salad with sliced oranges, black olives, and a tangy balsamic vinaigrette is terrific alongside.

Heat 2 tablespoons oil in heavy large pot over medium-high heat. Add bread and 1 teaspoon thyme; cook until bread is golden on both sides, turning with tongs, about 2 minutes total. Transfer croutons to bowl; sprinkle with salt and pepper.

Add remaining 4 tablespoons oil, garlic, and crushed red pepper to same pot; sauté over medium heat 30 seconds. Add kale and broth; bring to boil. Reduce heat to medium-low, cover, and simmer until kale wilts, about 5 minutes. Add tomatoes with juice, beans, and remaining 1 tablespoon thyme. Cover and simmer 15 minutes. Season with salt and pepper. Ladle ragout into shallow bowls. Top with croutons and serve.

4 SERVINGS

Banana, Raisin, and Oatmeal Pancakes

  1 cup old-fashioned oats

  1 cup all purpose flour

 ¼ cup (packed) golden brown sugar

1½ teaspoons baking powder

 ½ teaspoon baking soda

 ¼ teaspoon ground cinnamon

 ¾ cup plain yogurt

 ¾ cup whole milk

  2 large eggs

 ½ teaspoon vanilla extract

  2 ripe bananas, mashed

  1 cup raisins

 ¼ cup (½ stick) unsalted butter, melted

    Additional melted butter

Whisk first 6 ingredients in medium bowl. Whisk yogurt, milk, eggs, and vanilla in another medium bowl to blend. Whisk dry ingredients into yogurt mixture just until blended. Fold in mashed bananas, raisins, and 1/4 cup melted butter.

Brush nonstick griddle or skillet with melted butter; heat over medium heat. Working in batches, pour batter by 1/3 cupfuls onto griddle. Cook pancakes until bubbles form on top and bottoms are golden brown, about 2 minutes. Turn pancakes over and cook until bottoms are golden brown, about 2 minutes.

MAKES ABOUT 12

These are great with maple syrup, honey, marmalade, or even cottage cheese.

Poached Eggs in Pipérade

- 2 tablespoons olive oil
- 1 small onion, coarsely chopped (about 1 1/4 cups)
- 1 cup coarsely chopped bell peppers (preferably a mix of red, yellow, and green)
- 3 garlic cloves, finely chopped
- 2 large plum tomatoes, seeded, coarsely chopped
- 4 large eggs
- 1/4 cup crumbled feta cheese (about 1 ounce)

Heat oil in heavy 10-inch skillet over medium heat. Add onion, bell peppers, and garlic; sauté until vegetables begin to soften, about 5 minutes. Add tomatoes and sauté until soft, about 3 minutes. Season to taste with salt and pepper. Spread mixture evenly in skillet. Carefully break eggs over vegetable mixture, spacing evenly. Sprinkle eggs with salt and pepper; cover skillet and reduce heat to low. Cook eggs until whites set but yolks are still soft, about 5 minutes.

Using wide spatula, transfer 2 eggs with vegetable mixture underneath to each plate. Spoon remaining vegetables around eggs. Sprinkle pipérade with feta cheese and serve.

2 SERVINGS

Pipérade is a dish from the Basque region of France that features tomatoes and green peppers cooked in olive oil. French country bread, and baby greens in a Sherry wine vinaigrette make ideal accompaniments.

Stir-Fried Tofu with Mushrooms, Sugar Snap Peas, and Green Onions

3 tablespoons soy sauce
1 tablespoon unseasoned rice vinegar
1 tablespoon honey
1 teaspoon oriental sesame oil
¼ teaspoon dried crushed red pepper
1 12-ounce package extra-firm tofu, drained, cut into ¾-inch cubes, patted dry with paper towels
¼ cup water
1 teaspoon cornstarch

2 tablespoons vegetable oil, divided
6 ounces fresh shiitake mushrooms, stemmed, caps quartered
8 ounces sugar snap peas, trimmed
4 garlic cloves, minced
1 tablespoon minced peeled fresh ginger
4 green onions, sliced on diagonal

Whisk first 5 ingredients in medium bowl to blend. Add tofu and stir to coat; let tofu marinate 30 minutes. Drain tofu, reserving marinade in small bowl. Whisk ¼ cup water and cornstarch into marinade.

Heat 1 tablespoon vegetable oil in large nonstick skillet over medium-high heat. Add tofu and sauté until golden, about 2 minutes. Using slotted spoon, transfer tofu to plate. Add remaining 1 tablespoon vegetable oil to skillet. Add mushrooms and stir-fry until tender, about 3 minutes. Add sugar snap peas; stir-fry 2 minutes. Add garlic and ginger; stir-fry 30 seconds. Return tofu to skillet; drizzle reserved marinade mixture over. Stir-fry until marinade thickens slightly, about 30 seconds. Season to taste with salt and pepper. Transfer to bowl. Sprinkle with green onions and serve.

4 SERVINGS

Scrambled Eggs with Poblano Chiles and Cheese

  6 tablespoons (¾ stick) butter, divided
  1 cup chopped onion
  2 garlic cloves, chopped
  ½ teaspoon dried oregano
  1 14½-ounce can petite diced tomatoes in juice
  ¼ teaspoon chili powder

  2 large poblano chiles,* seeded, diced
  ½ cup chopped green onions
  ½ cup chopped fresh cilantro, divided
  8 large eggs, beaten to blend
  1 cup crumbled queso fresco or feta cheese (about 4 ounces)

Melt 2 tablespoons butter in large saucepan over medium heat. Add onion, garlic, and oregano and sauté until onion is soft, about 3 minutes. Add tomatoes with juice and chili powder. Cover and simmer 5 minutes to blend flavors. Transfer sauce to blender; puree until smooth. Season with salt and pepper. Return sauce to pan and keep warm.

Melt remaining 4 tablespoons butter in large skillet over medium heat. Add chiles; sauté until tender, about 6 minutes. Add green onions and ¼ cup cilantro. Add eggs and cheese. Cook until eggs are softly set, stirring occasionally, about 4 minutes. Divide eggs among 4 plates. Spoon sauce over; sprinkle with remaining ¼ cup cilantro.

A fresh green chile, often called a pasilla, available at some supermarkets and Latin American markets.

4 SERVINGS

Sunday Brunch for 4

Watermelon and Strawberry Smoothie
(page 41)

Coffee

Scrambled Eggs with Poblano Chiles and Cheese
(at left)

Warm Tortillas

Fruit Salad

Black Bean Chili

¼	cup olive oil
2	cups chopped onions
1⅔	cups coarsely chopped red bell peppers (about 2 medium)
6	garlic cloves, chopped
2	tablespoons chili powder
2	teaspoons dried oregano
1½	teaspoons ground cumin
½	teaspoon cayenne pepper
3	15- to 16-ounce cans black beans, drained, ½ cup liquid reserved
1	16-ounce can tomato sauce

Chopped fresh cilantro
Sour cream
Grated Monterey Jack cheese
Chopped green onions

Heat oil in heavy large pot over medium-high heat. Add onions, bell peppers, and garlic; sauté until onions soften, about 10 minutes. Mix in chili powder, oregano, cumin, and cayenne; stir 2 minutes. Mix in beans, ½ cup reserved bean liquid, and tomato sauce. Bring chili to boil, stirring occasionally. Reduce heat to medium-low and simmer until flavors blend and chili thickens, stirring occasionally, about 15 minutes. Season to taste with salt and pepper.

Ladle chili into bowls. Pass chopped cilantro, sour cream, grated cheese, and chopped green onions separately.

4 SERVINGS

Toasted Almond and Pecorino Sandwiches

3	cups whole unblanched almonds (about 1 pound), toasted, cooled
½	cup plus 2 tablespoons olive oil
3	tablespoons fresh lemon juice
1	tablespoon grated lemon peel
1	tablespoon chopped fresh sage
½	teaspoon salt
¼	teaspoon ground black pepper
12	½-inch-thick slices country-style bread (each about 3½x5½ inches)
1	10- to 12-ounce wedge Pecorino Romano cheese, cut into very thin slices
	Additional olive oil

Coarsely chop nuts in processor. Add next 6 ingredients. Blend until mixture forms coarse paste. *(Can be made 3 days ahead. Cover and chill. Let stand at room temperature 1 hour before using.)*

Divide almond paste among half of bread slices; spread to cover. Top with cheese. Sprinkle with pepper. Cover with remaining bread slices. Brush tops with oil.

Heat 2 large nonstick skillets over medium-high heat. Add 3 sandwiches, oiled side down, to each skillet. Cook until bread is crusty on bottom, about 6 minutes. Brush tops with oil. Turn sandwiches over. Cook until brown and crusty on bottom, pressing to compact, about 6 minutes and serve.

MAKES 6

Exactly what a fancy grilled cheese should be— top-notch cheese and bread with a little surprise (an almond-sage spread).

Yellow Squash and Mozzarella Quiche with Fresh Thyme

CRUST

1¼ cups unbleached all purpose flour

½ teaspoon salt

½ cup (1 stick) chilled unsalted butter, cut into ½-inch cubes

4 tablespoons (or more) ice water

FILLING

1 tablespoon butter

12 ounces yellow crookneck squash, cut into ¼-inch-thick rounds

2 teaspoons chopped fresh thyme

6 large eggs

1 cup whipping cream

¾ teaspoon salt

¼ teaspoon ground black pepper

¼ teaspoon hot pepper sauce

¾ cup (packed) coarsely grated mozzarella cheese (about 3 ounces)

FOR CRUST: Blend flour and salt in processor. Add butter. Using on/off turns, blend until coarse meal forms. Add 4 tablespoons ice water. Using on/off turns, blend until dough comes together in moist clumps, adding more ice water by teaspoonfuls if dough is dry. Gather dough into ball; flatten into disk. Wrap and chill at least 1 hour and up to 1 day.

Preheat oven to 375°F. Roll out dough on floured surface to 14½-inch round. Transfer to 10-inch-diameter tart pan with removable bottom. Fold overhang in; press to form double-thick sides. Push sides up until ¼ inch higher than top edge of pan. Pierce crust all over with fork. Freeze 10 minutes.

Line dough with foil and dried beans or pie weights. Bake until sides are set, about 25 minutes. Remove foil and beans. Bake until crust is golden, piercing with fork if crust bubbles, about 15 minutes. Transfer crust to rack; cool. Reduce oven temperature to 350°F.

FOR FILLING: Melt butter in heavy medium skillet over medium heat. Add squash and thyme. Sauté until squash is just tender, about 5 minutes. Cool to room temperature.

Whisk eggs, cream, salt, pepper, and hot sauce in bowl. Arrange squash over bottom of crust. Sprinkle with mozzarella. Place tart pan on oven rack. Pour egg mixture into crust, filling completely (some egg mixture may be left over).

Bake quiche until filling is golden and set in center, about 35 minutes. Transfer quiche to rack; cool 15 minutes.

4 SERVINGS

Open-Face Wild Mushroom and Fontina Sandwiches

- 1 pound mixed fresh shiitake, chanterelle, and porcini mushrooms
- 5 tablespoons olive oil
- 1 teaspoon minced fresh rosemary
- 2 medium shallots, minced
- 1 teaspoon minced fresh thyme
- ¼ cup Marsala

- 4 ½- to ¾-inch-thick center-cut slices country-style French bread
- 6 ounces imported Italian Fontina cheese, coarsely grated
- 2 tablespoons minced fresh parsley

Stem shiitake mushrooms. Cut all mushrooms lengthwise into ½-inch-thick slices. Heat olive oil in large nonstick skillet over medium-high heat. Add rosemary and stir 10 seconds, then add mushrooms. Sprinkle with salt and pepper. Sauté until mushrooms begin to brown, about 10 minutes. Add shallots and thyme; stir 2 minutes. Add Marsala and boil until evaporated, about 30 seconds. Remove from heat. Season with salt and pepper. *(Can be prepared 1 hour ahead. Let stand at room temperature.)*

Preheat broiler. Place bread slices on baking sheet; broil until lightly toasted, about 2 minutes per side. Divide cheese among bread slices, covering completely. Broil until cheese melts, about 2 minutes. Rewarm mushrooms over medium heat if necessary. Mix in parsley. Place toasts on plates. Spoon mushrooms over and serve.

MAKES 4

Roasted Bell Pepper Halves Stuffed with Bulgur and Spinach

3	red bell peppers (2 large and 1 small)
2	large yellow bell peppers
2	tablespoons olive oil, divided
2	cups water
1	cup coarse or medium bulgur*
1	teaspoon salt
¼	cup dried currants
2	tablespoons pine nuts
2	teaspoons ground cumin
1	6-ounce bag fresh baby spinach leaves
3	tablespoons chopped fresh mint
3	tablespoons chopped fresh dill
1	cup crumbled feta cheese (about 4 ounces), divided

Preheat oven to 425°F. Cut large red and yellow bell peppers in half through stem end. Remove seeds and cut out ribs, leaving stems intact. Finely chop small red bell pepper; set aside. Spread 1 tablespoon oil over rimmed baking sheet. Place pepper halves, cut side down, on prepared sheet. Roast 15 minutes. Turn over; roast until slightly softened, about 15 minutes longer. Remove from oven.

Meanwhile, bring 2 cups water to boil in medium saucepan; add bulgur and 1 teaspoon salt. Remove from heat. Cover and let stand until bulgur is tender, about 30 minutes. Drain well.

Heat 1 tablespoon oil in large skillet over medium-high heat. Add chopped red pepper; sauté until tender, about 3 minutes. Add currants and pine nuts; sauté 2 minutes. Add cumin; stir 20 seconds. Mix in spinach; stir until beginning to wilt, about 2 minutes. Remove from heat. Mix in bulgur, mint, and dill. Stir in half of cheese. Season with salt and pepper. Divide bulgur mixture among pepper halves. Sprinkle with remaining cheese. (*Can be made 1 day ahead. Cover and chill.*)

Preheat oven to 425°F. Bake stuffed peppers until heated through, about 25 minutes (or 30 minutes if chilled); serve.

Bulgur, also called cracked wheat, is available at supermarkets and natural foods stores.

4 SERVINGS

Post-Hike Lunch for 4

Crudités

Open-Face Wild Mushroom and Fontina Sandwiches
(opposite, pictured opposite)

Mixed Green Salad

Iced Tea

Fruit and Nut Cereal Cookies
(page 230)

Strawberries

Goat Cheese, Sun-Dried Tomato, and Roasted Garlic Soufflés

- 6 large garlic cloves, flattened
- 1 teaspoon olive oil
- 1 teaspoon salt
- ¾ teaspoon ground black pepper

  Nonstick vegetable oil spray
- 4 tablespoons plain dry breadcrumbs
- 1 tablespoon butter
- 2 tablespoons all purpose flour
- 1¼ cups low-fat (1%) milk
- ½ cup finely chopped drained oil-packed sun-dried tomatoes
- 2½ teaspoons chopped fresh thyme

- 4 large egg yolks
- 4 ounces mild fresh goat cheese, crumbled (about 1 cup)
- 6 large egg whites
- ⅛ teaspoon cream of tartar

Preheat oven to 350°F. Combine garlic and oil in small custard cup. Cover with foil. Bake until garlic is very tender, about 35 minutes. Cool slightly. Add 1 teaspoon salt and ¾ teaspoon pepper to custard cup and mash to paste. Maintain oven temperature.

Spray four 2-cup soufflé dishes with nonstick spray. Sprinkle each with 1 tablespoon breadcrumbs, coating bottom and sides; place dishes on baking sheet. Melt butter in medium saucepan over medium heat. Add flour; whisk until smooth, about 1 minute. Gradually add milk, whisking constantly until mixture boils, thickens, and is smooth, about 2 minutes. Stir in tomatoes, thyme, and garlic mixture. Remove soufflé base from heat.

Whisk egg yolks in large bowl to blend. Gradually whisk in hot soufflé base, then fold in goat cheese. Using electric mixer, beat egg whites in another large bowl until foamy. Add cream of tartar; beat until stiff but not dry. Fold whites into soufflé mixture in 4 additions. Divide among prepared dishes.

Bake until puffed and golden, about 25 minutes. Serve immediately.

4 SERVINGS

Grilled Pitas with Tomatoes, Olives, and Feta

1 cup diced seeded plum tomatoes (about 4)
½ cup pitted coarsely chopped mixed olives
½ cup chopped red onion
4 tablespoons olive oil, divided
3 tablespoons chopped fresh mint

4 whole wheat pita breads
½ cup crumbled feta cheese (about 3 ounces)

Pita bread serves as the crust for this pizza-style dish. Look for prepackaged mixed black and green brine-cured olives in the deli section of most supermarkets. Partner this with tabbouleh (bulgur salad), arugula salad with red wine vinaigrette, and marinated artichoke hearts.

Prepare barbecue (medium-high heat). Stir tomatoes, olives, onion, 2 tablespoons oil, and mint in small bowl to blend.

Brush 1 side of each pita with remaining 2 tablespoons oil; place pitas, oiled side down, on grill. Cook until lightly charred, about 2 minutes. Turn pitas over; top with tomato mixture, spreading almost to edges. Sprinkle with cheese.

Cover barbecue and grill pitas until topping is warm, about 2 minutes. Transfer pitas to plates and serve.

4 SERVINGS

Smoked Cheese and Sausage Lasagna

SAUCE

- 3 tablespoons olive oil, divided
- 1 pound Italian sweet sausages, casings removed
- 2 ounces sliced prosciutto, chopped

- 2 cups chopped onions
- 1 celery stalk, chopped
- 3 garlic cloves, chopped
- 1 teaspoon dried oregano
- ¼ teaspoon dried crushed red pepper
- 2 tablespoons tomato paste
- 1 28-ounce can Italian-style tomatoes in juice, tomatoes chopped, juice reserved
- 2 tablespoons chopped fresh basil

LASAGNA

- 12 10x2-inch lasagna noodles
- 1 15-ounce container whole-milk ricotta cheese
- 2 cups (packed) coarsely grated smoked mozzarella cheese, divided
- 1 large egg

  Olive oil

FOR SAUCE: Heat 1 tablespoon oil in large saucepan over medium-high heat. Add sausage; sauté until browned, breaking up with fork, about 6 minutes. Add prosciutto; stir 1 minute. Transfer mixture to bowl.

Heat 2 tablespoons oil in same pan over medium-high heat. Add onions and next 4 ingredients. Sauté until tender, about 5 minutes. Stir in tomato paste. Add tomatoes with reserved juice, basil, and sausage mixture. Reduce heat; simmer until sauce thickens, stirring occasionally, about 15 minutes. Season with salt and pepper. *(Can be made 1 day ahead. Cover and refrigerate.)*

FOR LASAGNA: Cook noodles in large pot of boiling salted water until just tender but still firm to bite. Drain. Arrange in single layer on baking sheet. Stir ricotta and 1½ cups mozzarella in bowl. Season with salt and pepper; mix in egg.

Brush 13x9x2-inch glass baking dish with oil. Spread 1 cup tomato sauce evenly over bottom. Arrange 3 noodles atop sauce. Spread ¾ cup cheese mixture thinly over noodles. Spoon 1½ cups sauce over. Repeat with noodles, cheese mixture, and sauce 2 more times. Cover with 3 noodles. Sprinkle with remaining ½ cup mozzarella. Cover with foil. *(Can be prepared 1 day ahead. Chill.)*

Preheat oven to 350°F. Bake lasagna, covered, 40 minutes. Uncover and bake 15 minutes longer. Let stand 10 minutes and serve.

8 SERVINGS

Linguine with Mushrooms and Parmesan Cream Sauce

¼ cup olive oil
1½ pounds crimini mushrooms, sliced
 6 large garlic cloves, thinly sliced
⅛ teaspoon ground nutmeg
1¼ cups whipping cream

16 ounces linguine
3½ cups grated Parmesan cheese, divided
¾ cup chopped fresh parsley, divided

Heat oil in large skillet over medium-high heat. Add mushrooms, garlic, and nutmeg; sauté until mushrooms are brown and tender, about 10 minutes. Sprinkle with salt and pepper. Stir in cream. Remove mushroom mixture from heat.

Cook pasta in large pot of boiling salted water until tender but still firm to bite. Drain, reserving ½ cup cooking liquid. Return pasta to pot. Add mushroom mixture, 2½ cups cheese, ½ cup parsley, and reserved cooking liquid. Toss over medium-high heat until sauce coats pasta. Season with salt and pepper. Mix in remaining ¼ cup parsley. Transfer pasta to bowl. Serve with remaining cheese.

4 TO 6 SERVINGS

**Friday Night Dinner
and a Movie for 8**

**Roasted Red Peppers,
Peperoncini, and Olives**

Breadsticks

**Smoked Cheese and
Sausage Lasagna**
(opposite, pictured opposite)

Caesar Salad

Chianti

Ice Cream Truffles
(page 214)

Baked Ziti with Spicy Pork and Sausage Ragù

2 tablespoons olive oil

4 ounces thinly sliced pancetta (Italian bacon), chopped

2 pounds Boston butt (pork shoulder), cut into 1¼-inch cubes

1 pound Italian hot sausages, casings removed

2 cups chopped onions

¾ cup chopped carrots

¾ cup chopped celery

6 large fresh thyme sprigs

6 large garlic cloves, chopped

2 bay leaves

½ teaspoon dried crushed red pepper

2 cups dry red wine

1 28-ounce can plum tomatoes in juice, tomatoes chopped, juice reserved

1¼ pounds ziti pasta

2 cups (packed) coarsely grated whole-milk mozzarella cheese (about 8 ounces)

½ cup freshly grated Parmesan cheese

Heat olive oil in heavy large pot over medium-high heat. Add pancetta and sauté until brown and crisp. Using slotted spoon, transfer pancetta to bowl. Sprinkle pork with salt and pepper. Add half of pork to drippings in pot; sauté until brown, about 7 minutes. Transfer to bowl with pancetta. Repeat with remaining pork. Add sausage to same pot. Sauté until no longer pink, breaking up with back of fork, about 5 minutes. Add onions, carrots, celery, thyme, garlic, bay leaves, and crushed red pepper. Reduce heat to medium-low; sauté until vegetables are tender, about 10 minutes. Add wine and bring to boil, scraping up browned bits. Add pancetta and pork with any accumulated juices; boil 2 minutes. Add tomatoes with juice.

Cover and cook until pork is very tender, adjusting heat as needed to maintain gentle simmer and stirring occasionally, about 2 hours.

Uncover pot; tilt to 1 side and spoon off fat from surface of ragù. Gently press pork pieces with back of fork to break up meat coarsely. Season ragù to taste with salt and pepper. *(Can be made 2 days ahead. Cool slightly. Refrigerate uncovered until cold, then cover and keep refrigerated. Rewarm over low heat before continuing.)*

Preheat oven to 400°F. Butter 15x10x2-inch glass baking dish or other 4-quart baking dish. Cook pasta in large pot of boiling salted water until tender but still firm to bite, stirring occasionally. Drain pasta; mix into ragù. Season mixture to taste with salt and pepper; transfer to prepared dish. Sprinkle both cheeses over. Bake until heated through and golden, about 20 minutes.

8 SERVINGS

Braised pork shoulder, spicy Italian sausage, and pancetta enrich the tomato sauce. Dried crushed red pepper kicks up the heat.

Tagliatelle with Shredded Beets, Sour Cream, and Parsley

- 1 tablespoon butter
- 2 tablespoons olive oil
- 2 garlic cloves, minced
- 3 cups (packed) coarsely grated peeled uncooked beets (about 3 large)
- ½ teaspoon cayenne pepper
- 2 tablespoons fresh lemon juice

- 12 ounces tagliatelle or fettuccine

- 1 8-ounce container sour cream
- 6 tablespoons chopped fresh Italian parsley, divided

Sour cream and beets are inseparable in Eastern European cooking. Here's a fresh new way to enjoy them together.

Melt butter with oil in large nonstick skillet over medium heat. Add garlic; stir until pale golden, about 1 minute. Add beets and cayenne; reduce heat to medium-low and sauté just until beets are tender, about 12 minutes. Stir in lemon juice.

Meanwhile, cook pasta in large pot of boiling salted water until tender but still firm to bite, stirring occasionally.

Drain pasta and return to pot. Stir in sour cream and 4 tablespoons parsley, then beet mixture. Season to taste with salt and pepper. Transfer pasta to bowl. Sprinkle with remaining 2 tablespoons parsley and serve.

4 SERVINGS

Crispy Noodle Cake with Barbecued Pork

- 1 tablespoon cornstarch
- 1 tablespoon cold water
- 2 tablespoons soy sauce
- 1 tablespoon sugar
- 1 tablespoon oriental sesame oil

- 2 cups mung bean sprouts
- 8 ounces dried Chinese egg noodles*

- 4 tablespoons peanut oil, divided
- 2 tablespoons minced peeled fresh ginger
- 2 garlic cloves, minced
- 2 large green onions, white and pale green parts minced, tops cut into 1-inch pieces
- 2 medium carrots, cut into matchstick-size strips
- 4 ounces snow peas, cut on diagonal into matchstick-size strips
- 6 ounces Chinese barbecued pork, cut into matchstick-size strips**

Stir cornstarch and 1 tablespoon cold water in small bowl to blend. Mix in soy sauce, sugar, and sesame oil.

Blanch bean sprouts in large pot of boiling salted water 10 seconds. Using large slotted skimmer or sieve, transfer sprouts to colander. Rinse under cold water to cool quickly. Add noodles to same pot of boiling water and cook until just tender but still firm to bite, about 5 minutes. Drain well; rinse with cold water and drain again, tossing to release as much water as possible.

Heat 1 tablespoon peanut oil in heavy large wok or skillet over medium-high heat. Add ginger, garlic, and minced green onions. Sauté 1 minute. Add carrots, snow peas, and pork. Stir-fry until carrots are just crisp-tender, about 2 minutes. Mix in bean sprouts, noodles, and green onion tops. Stir-fry 1 minute. Stir cornstarch mixture to reblend and add to wok. Cook until sauce thickens, stirring often, about 2 minutes. Season with salt and pepper. Transfer noodle mixture to large bowl and cool.

(Can be made 2 hours ahead. Let stand at room temperature.)

Heat 2 tablespoons peanut oil in heavy large nonstick skillet over medium heat. Add noodle mixture. Cook until bottom of noodle cake is brown and crusty, occasionally pressing to compact and shaking pan to prevent sticking, about 5 minutes. Turn cake out onto rimless baking sheet, browned side up. Add remaining 1 tablespoon oil to skillet and heat. Slide noodle cake back into skillet, browned side up. Cook until bottom is brown and crusty, about 6 minutes. Slide noodle cake out onto platter. Cut into wedges and serve.

*Thin, spaghetti-like noodles, available in the Asian foods section of many supermarkets and at Asian markets.
**Available at Chinese delicatessens.

4 SERVINGS

Pasta with Lemon, Spinach, Parmesan, and Breadcrumbs

> Mung bean sprouts, commonly known simply as bean sprouts, are available in the produce section of most supermarkets.

2 cups fresh breadcrumbs made from crustless French bread

7 tablespoons extra-virgin olive oil, divided

12 ounces linguine

4 garlic cloves, thinly sliced

3 tablespoons fresh lemon juice

¼ teaspoon dried crushed red pepper

1 6-ounce bag baby spinach leaves
    Grated Parmesan cheese

Preheat oven to 375°F. Toss breadcrumbs with 1 tablespoon oil in large bowl to coat. Spread evenly on rimmed baking sheet. Bake until breadcrumbs are golden, about 5 minutes. Cool. Sprinkle with salt.

Cook pasta in large pot of boiling salted water until tender but still firm to bite, stirring occasionally. Drain, reserving ½ cup cooking liquid.

Meanwhile, heat remaining 6 tablespoons olive oil, thinly sliced garlic, lemon juice, and dried crushed red pepper in heavy small saucepan over medium heat. Cook oil mixture until garlic turns golden, about 5 minutes.

Toss pasta, oil mixture, and spinach in large bowl until spinach wilts, adding reserved cooking liquid as needed to moisten. Sprinkle breadcrumbs over. Serve pasta, passing grated Parmesan cheese separately.

4 SERVINGS

Orecchiette with Spiced Duck Ragù

    4   tablespoons extra-virgin olive oil
    2   breast halves and 2 leg-thigh pieces from one 4½-pound duck, skinned; or 2 pounds
        chicken thighs with bones, skinned
   ¼   cup coarsely chopped fresh basil
    3   garlic cloves, chopped
    1   tablespoon chopped fresh thyme
   ½   cinnamon stick
   ½   teaspoon dried crushed red pepper
   3½   cups canned crushed tomatoes or canned tomato puree (from two 28-ounce cans)

   12   ounces orecchiette (little ear-shaped pasta)
    1   cup coarsely chopped arugula
    2   tablespoons freshly grated Parmesan cheese
   ½   cup ¼-inch-dice feta cheese

Heat oil in heavy large pot over medium-high heat. Sprinkle duck with salt and pepper. Add duck to pot and sauté until brown, about 3 minutes per side. Transfer duck to plate. Add basil, garlic, thyme, cinnamon stick, and crushed red pepper to pot; sauté 3 minutes. Return duck to pot. Add tomatoes; bring to boil. Reduce heat to medium-low, cover, and simmer until duck is tender, about 1 hour. Remove cinnamon stick. Transfer duck to

work surface. Cut all meat from bones; cut meat into strips. Return meat to pot. Season duck ragù to taste with salt and pepper. (*Can be prepared 1 day ahead. Cool slightly. Chill uncovered until cold, then cover and keep chilled. Rewarm over medium heat before serving.*)

Cook orecchiette in large pot of boiling salted water until just tender but still firm to bite. Drain pasta. Return to pot. Add duck ragù, arugula, and Parmesan cheese; toss to blend. Divide pasta among small bowls. Sprinkle with feta cheese.

2 TO 4 SERVINGS

Penne with Pancetta and Tomato-Cream Sauce

½ cup chopped pancetta (Italian bacon) or bacon (3 ounces)
1 tablespoon olive oil
2 garlic cloves, finely chopped
2 14½-ounce cans petite diced tomatoes in juice
½ cup dry white wine
½ cup whipping cream
¾ cup torn basil leaves, divided

1 pound penne

Using the fresh-tasting canned diced tomatoes eliminates the chopping step. Offer arugula and radicchio salad alongside the pasta.

Cook pancetta in large skillet over medium-low heat until crisp, about 8 minutes. Using slotted spoon, transfer pancetta to paper towels to drain. Add olive oil and garlic to pancetta drippings and sauté 30 seconds. Add tomatoes with juice, wine, and cream. Bring sauce to boil; reduce heat to medium and simmer until sauce is slightly reduced, about 10 minutes. Stir in ½ cup basil. Season with salt and pepper.

Meanwhile, cook pasta in pot of boiling salted water until tender but still firm to bite. Drain pasta and divide among 4 bowls. Spoon sauce over pasta. Sprinkle with pancetta and remaining ¼ cup basil.

4 SERVINGS

Gemelli with Zucchini, Tomatoes, and Bacon

12 bacon slices, cut crosswise into 1-inch pieces
 1 large red onion, chopped (about 2 cups)
1½ cups dry white wine

12 ounces gemelli or rotini (about 3 cups)
 3 slender zucchini, halved lengthwise and sliced crosswise into
   ½-inch-wide pieces

 3 large plum tomatoes, seeded, coarsely chopped (about 1½ cups)
⅓ cup chopped fresh oregano
 1 cup crumbled soft fresh goat cheese (about 4 ounces)

Cook bacon in heavy large skillet over medium-high heat until brown and crisp. Using slotted spoon, transfer to paper towels to drain. Pour off all but 3 tablespoons drippings from skillet. Add onion and sauté until soft, about 3 minutes. Add wine; boil until reduced by ⅓, about 3 minutes.

Meanwhile, cook pasta in large pot of boiling salted water until slightly underdone. Add zucchini and boil until pasta is tender but still firm to bite and zucchini is crisp-tender, stirring occasionally, about 2 minutes longer. Drain.

Add pasta, zucchini, bacon, tomatoes, and oregano to onion in skillet. Toss over medium-high heat until sauce coats pasta, about 3 minutes. Add cheese and toss until beginning to melt, about 2 minutes. Season to taste with salt and pepper and serve.

6 SERVINGS

Stir-Fried Noodles
with Singapore Lamb Curry

  8 ounces dried chow mein udon noodles (Asian-style spaghetti)*
  3 tablespoons vegetable oil, divided
  2 tablespoons dry Sherry
  1 teaspoon cornstarch
  2 tablespoons soy sauce
  1 tablespoon mild-flavored (light) molasses
  2 tablespoons canned unsweetened coconut milk*
  2 teaspoons curry powder
  1 teaspoon chili-garlic sauce*

  3 tablespoons finely chopped peeled fresh ginger
  2 large garlic cloves, minced
  2 green onions, cut into 1-inch pieces
  2 jalapeño chiles, seeded, chopped
  8 ounces leg of lamb meat, cut into 1x½x¼-inch strips
  2 cups thinly sliced Napa cabbage
  ¾ cup matchstick-size strips red bell pepper
  ¾ cup matchstick-size strips green bell pepper
  4 tablespoons finely chopped fresh cilantro, divided

Cook noodles in large pot of boiling salted water until just tender but still firm to bite, stirring occasionally. Drain. Return to pot and mix in 1 tablespoon oil. Stir Sherry and cornstarch in small bowl to blend. Mix in next 5 ingredients.

Heat 2 tablespoons oil in large nonstick skillet over high heat. Add ginger, garlic, green onions, and chiles. Sauté until fragrant, about 1 minute. Add lamb, cabbage, and all bell peppers. Stir-fry until lamb is just cooked through, about 2 minutes. Stir Sherry seasoning mixture and add; simmer until sauce thickens, stirring often, about 2 minutes. Add lamb sauce to noodles in pot. Toss over medium-high heat until noodles are heated and coated with sauce, about 2 minutes. Mix in 2 tablespoons cilantro. Transfer to bowl. Sprinkle with remaining 2 tablespoons cilantro.

*Available in the Asian foods section of most supermarkets and at Asian markets.

4 SERVINGS

Farfalle with Mascarpone, Asparagus, and Hazelnuts

2 pounds slender asparagus, trimmed, cut on diagonal into 2-inch
    lengths (about 6 cups)
3 tablespoons olive oil

1 pound farfalle (bow-tie pasta)
1 8-ounce container mascarpone cheese*
²⁄₃ cup freshly grated Parmesan cheese

½ cup hazelnuts, toasted, husked, coarsely chopped
3 tablespoons chopped fresh chives
    Parmesan cheese shavings

Preheat oven to 450°F. Line rimmed baking sheet with aluminum foil. Place asparagus on prepared sheet. Drizzle with olive oil and sprinkle with salt and pepper. Toss to coat; spread in single layer. Roast until asparagus is tender, about 10 minutes. (*Can be prepared 2 hours ahead; let stand at room temperature.*)

Cook pasta in large pot of boiling salted water until tender but still firm to bite, stirring occasionally. Drain, reserving 1 cup pasta cooking water. Return pasta to pot. Stir in mascarpone, grated Parmesan cheese, and asparagus. Toss over medium-low heat until pasta is coated with sauce and mixture is heated through, adding reserved pasta water by ¼ cupfuls if dry, about 3 minutes.

Mound pasta in large shallow serving bowl. Sprinkle with hazelnuts, chives, and Parmesan cheese shavings.

Mascarpone, Italian cream cheese, is available in some supermarkets and Italian markets.

4 SERVINGS

Pasta Party for 4

Bruschetta

Farfalle with Mascarpone, Asparagus, and Hazelnuts
(at left, pictured opposite)

Arugula Salad

Pinot Grigio

Pink Grapefruit, Strawberry, and Champagne Granita with Sugared Strawberries
(page 217)

Tricolor Tomato Fettuccine

⅔ cup olive oil, divided
6 large shallots, thinly sliced
4 large garlic cloves, thinly sliced
4 pounds red, yellow, and green heirloom tomatoes, seeded, coarsely chopped (about 6½ cups)
½ cup thinly sliced fresh basil
2 tablespoons chopped fresh oregano

12 ounces fettuccine
2 ounces shaved Parmesan cheese

Heat ⅓ cup oil in large skillet over medium-high heat. Add shallots; sauté 5 minutes. Add garlic; sauté 2 minutes. Reduce heat to medium; add tomatoes and herbs. Stir until tomatoes are heated through, about 2 minutes. Remove from heat; season with salt and pepper.

Meanwhile, cook pasta in large pot of boiling salted water until tender but still firm to bite. Drain; transfer to bowl. Top with tomato mixture. Drizzle with ⅓ cup oil and sprinkle with Parmesan.

4 SERVINGS

Pasta with Pesto, Broccoli, and Potatoes

4 red-skinned potatoes, peeled (about ½ pound)
1 pound broccoli, cut into 2-inch pieces
1 pound linguine
1 cup purchased pesto
    Freshly grated Parmesan cheese

Cook potatoes in large pot of boiling salted water until tender, about 10 minutes. Using slotted spoon, transfer potatoes to cutting board; return water to boil. Add broccoli; cook 3 minutes. Using slotted spoon, transfer broccoli to large bowl; return water to boil. Add linguine and cook until tender but still firm to bite, stirring occasionally. Drain, reserving ½ cup cooking water. Cut potatoes into small chunks. Add potatoes, pasta, and pesto to broccoli and toss, adding reserved cooking water by tablespoonfuls to moisten if necessary. Season with salt and pepper. Serve, passing cheese separately.

6 SERVINGS

Tarragon Pizza Bianca

2 10-ounce tubes refrigerated pizza dough
6 tablespoons extra-virgin olive oil
4 teaspoons chopped fresh tarragon
1⅓ cups (packed) grated whole-milk mozzarella cheese
1 medium fennel bulb, trimmed, very thinly sliced
1 small zucchini, very thinly sliced
1 small yellow crookneck squash, very thinly sliced
2 tablespoons minced shallot
4 ounces Brie, rind removed, cheese cut into ½-inch cubes

Position rack in bottom third of oven; preheat to 425°F. Oil baking sheet. Unroll dough onto floured surface. Cut each rectangle in half. Roll each half to 7-inch round. Transfer rounds to prepared baking sheet. Brush 1 tablespoon oil over each round; sprinkle each with 1 teaspoon tarragon. Top with mozzarella and vegetables. Brush rounds with remaining oil. Sprinkle with shallot, salt, and pepper. Top with Brie. Bake until cheese is bubbling, about 14 minutes. Cut each into 4 wedges.

4 SERVINGS

Wild Mushroom Pizza with Caramelized Onions, Fontina, and Rosemary

7   tablespoons butter, divided
2   tablespoons plus 1 teaspoon grapeseed oil
3   onions, halved lengthwise, thinly sliced crosswise (about 6 cups)

2   pounds assorted wild mushrooms (such as crimini, oyster, chanterelle, and stemmed shiitake), cut into bite-size pieces
6   garlic cloves, minced
2   tablespoons minced shallot (about 1 medium)
2   cups dry white wine
1   tablespoon minced fresh rosemary

   Pizza Dough (see recipe)
   Cornmeal (for dusting)
   Garlic oil
3   cups grated Fontina cheese (about 10 ounces)

Melt 3 tablespoons butter with 2 tablespoons grapeseed oil in heavy large skillet over medium heat. Add onions; sauté until golden, about 45 minutes. Season with salt and pepper.

Melt remaining 4 tablespoons butter with 1 teaspoon grapeseed oil in another heavy large skillet over medium-high heat. Add mushrooms, garlic, and shallot. Sauté 4 minutes. Add wine and simmer until almost all liquid is absorbed, stirring frequently, about 13 minutes. Add rosemary; season with salt and pepper.

Position rack in bottom third of oven. Place heavy 17x11-inch baking sheet on rack (invert if rimmed). Preheat oven to 500°F at least 30 minutes before baking. Roll out 2 dough disks on lightly floured surface to 8-inch rounds, allowing dough to rest a few minutes if it springs back. Sprinkle another baking sheet (invert if rimmed) with cornmeal. Transfer 1 dough round to second baking sheet. Lightly brush dough with garlic oil. Sprinkle with 1/2 cup cheese. Scatter 2 1/2 tablespoons onions over cheese. Scatter 1/2 cup mushrooms over onions. Sprinkle with salt.

Position baking sheet with pizza at far edge of 1 side of hot baking sheet. Tilt sheet and pull back slowly, allowing pizza to slide onto hot sheet. Repeat with second dough disk, garlic oil, cheese, onions, mushrooms, and salt, and slide second pizza onto second half of hot baking sheet. Bake pizzas 6 minutes. Rotate pizzas half a turn. Bake until crust is deep brown, about 6 minutes longer. Using large spatula, carefully transfer pizzas to cutting board. Let rest 1 minute. Slice into wedges and serve. Repeat with remaining ingredients.

MAKES SIX 8-INCH PIZZAS

Pizza Dough

- 1½ cups warm water (110°F to 115°F)
- 1½ tablespoons sugar
- 3 teaspoons active dry yeast (about 1½ envelopes)
- 4½ cups all purpose flour
- 4½ tablespoons olive oil
- 2¼ teaspoons salt

  Cornmeal (for dusting)
  Nonstick vegetable oil spray

Brush large bowl with oil. Mix warm water and sugar in processor. Sprinkle yeast over; stir to dissolve. Let stand until mixture bubbles, about 10 minutes. Add flour, 4½ tablespoons oil, and salt. Process 1 minute. Transfer dough to floured surface; knead until smooth, about 5 minutes. Transfer to prepared bowl, turning to coat with oil. Cover bowl with plastic wrap. Let dough rise in warm draft-free area until doubled, about 1 hour.

Sprinkle cornmeal over rimmed baking sheet. Divide dough into 6 equal portions; roll each into ball. Space dough balls evenly on baking sheet. Lightly spray large sheet of plastic with nonstick spray; place over dough, sprayed side down. Refrigerate 1 hour before rolling and baking.

MAKES 6 CRUSTS

Spiced Winter Squash with Fennel
(page 150)

On the Side

Side Dishes

Salads

Breads

Spinach and Roasted Red Pepper Gratin

4	10-ounce bags fresh spinach leaves
3	red bell peppers
1½	tablespoons butter
1½	tablespoons olive oil
3	medium leeks (white and pale green parts only), thinly sliced (about 3 cups)
1	large shallot, chopped (about ¼ cup)
3	garlic cloves, minced
1	cup whipping cream
4	large eggs
1	cup part-skim ricotta cheese
½	cup grated Swiss cheese
¼	cup grated Parmesan cheese
1½	teaspoons salt
½	teaspoon ground black pepper

Heat large deep nonstick skillet over medium-high heat. Working in batches (about 10 cups at a time), sauté fresh spinach in dry skillet until bright green and wilted, about 2 minutes per batch. Transfer spinach to strainer. Squeeze spinach dry; roll in kitchen towel to remove excess water.

Char peppers directly over gas flame or in broiler until blackened on all sides. Enclose in paper bag; let stand 10 minutes. Peel, seed, and slice peppers into 1/4-inch-wide strips.

Melt butter with oil in heavy large skillet over medium heat. Add leeks, shallot, and garlic; cook until soft, about 5 minutes. Remove from heat. Whisk cream and eggs in large bowl to blend. Whisk in all cheeses, salt, and pepper. Stir in spinach, leek mixture, and 2/3 of roasted red peppers (reserve 1/3 of peppers for topping). *(Can be prepared 1 day ahead. Cover and refrigerate.)*

Preheat oven to 350°F. Generously butter 13x9x2-inch baking dish. Transfer spinach mixture to prepared dish. Bake gratin until knife inserted into center comes out clean, about 50 minutes. Arrange remaining red pepper strips decoratively atop gratin and serve.

8 SERVINGS

Creamed spinach gets a makeover with three cheeses and a vibrant garnish.

Pancetta Green Beans

12 ounces green beans, trimmed

3 ounces pancetta (Italian bacon), coarsely chopped

1 tablespoon butter

Cook beans in large pot of boiling salted water until crisp-tender, about 4 minutes. Drain. Transfer to bowl of ice water; cool 5 minutes. Drain. Transfer beans to paper towels and pat dry.

Heat large skillet over medium heat. Add pancetta and sauté until crisp, about 3 minutes. Using slotted spoon, transfer to paper-towel-lined plate to drain. Increase heat to medium-high. Add butter to same skillet. Add beans and stir until heated through, about 4 minutes. Season with salt and pepper. Stir in pancetta.

4 SERVINGS

Coriander Rice

½ cup olive oil

1½ cups minced shallots (about 8)

3 tablespoons ground coriander

¾ teaspoon turmeric

4½ cups basmati rice or other long-grain white rice

9 cups low-salt chicken broth

3 teaspoons salt

½ cup chopped fresh Italian parsley

Heat oil in heavy large pot over medium heat. Add shallots and sauté until tender and golden brown, about 12 minutes. Add coriander and turmeric and stir 1 minute. Add rice and stir until coated. Add broth and salt; bring to simmer. Cover; reduce heat to low. Cook until rice is tender and liquid is absorbed, about 20 minutes. Stir in parsley. Transfer to platter and serve.

16 SERVINGS

Grilled Tomatoes Stuffed with Goat Cheese and Sage

2 tablespoons olive oil

4 tablespoons chopped fresh sage (about 1 ounce), divided

½ cup soft fresh goat cheese

2 teaspoons sliced green onions

1 shallot, minced

¼ teaspoon salt

4 medium heirloom tomatoes

Heat oil in medium skillet over medium-high heat. Add 3 tablespoons fresh sage and fry 30 seconds. Using slotted spoon, transfer fried sage to paper towel.

Combine cheese, onions, shallot, salt, and remaining 1 tablespoon fresh sage in bowl. Season with pepper. Using small sharp knife, remove cone-shaped piece 2 inches wide and 1 inch deep from top of each tomato. Divide cheese mixture among tomatoes; top with fried sage.

Prepare barbecue (medium-high heat). Place tomatoes on grill rack; cover barbecue with lid. Cook until tomatoes are soft, about 5 minutes.

4 SERVINGS

Lemon-Barley Pilaf

    1   tablespoon butter
    1   small onion, finely chopped
    ¾   cup pearl barley
    2   cups low-salt chicken broth
    1   bay leaf

    1   medium carrot, peeled, finely chopped
    ½   red bell pepper, finely chopped
    1   teaspoon grated lemon peel

Melt butter in heavy medium saucepan over medium heat. Add onion; sprinkle with salt and pepper. Sauté until onion is beginning to soften, about 5 minutes. Add barley; cook 3 minutes, stirring constantly. Add chicken broth and bay leaf; bring to boil. Reduce heat to low, stir once, and cover. Cook until barley is almost tender, about 25 minutes.

Add carrot and bell pepper; cover and cook until vegetables are tender, about 6 minutes. Remove pilaf from heat and stir. Cover and let stand 10 minutes. Discard bay leaf. Season to taste with salt and pepper. Stir in lemon peel and serve.

4 SERVINGS

Sautéed Radishes and Sugar Snap Peas with Dill

This side dish would pair beautifully with roast lamb or salmon. To remove strings from fresh peas, just snap off the stem end and pull string lengthwise down each pod.

    1   tablespoon butter
    1   tablespoon olive oil
    ½   cup thinly sliced shallots
    12 ounces sugar snap peas, trimmed, strings removed
    2   cups thinly sliced radishes (about 1 large bunch)
    ¼   cup orange juice
    1   teaspoon dill seeds
    1   tablespoon chopped fresh dill

Melt butter with oil in large nonstick skillet over medium heat. Add shallots and sauté until golden, about 5 minutes. Add sugar snap peas and radishes; sauté until crisp-tender, about 5 minutes. Add orange juice and dill seeds; stir 1 minute. Season with salt and pepper. Stir in chopped dill. Transfer to bowl; serve.

6 SERVINGS

Mixed Vegetable Sauté with Herbs and Garlic

3 large carrots, peeled, halved lengthwise, then cut on diagonal into ¼-inch-thick slices

5 tablespoons olive oil

6 garlic cloves, chopped

1½ tablespoons chopped fresh tarragon

1 tablespoon chopped fresh thyme

4 large red bell peppers, cut lengthwise into ½-inch-wide strips

4 large zucchini, halved lengthwise, then cut on diagonal into ½-inch-thick slices

4 large yellow crookneck squash, halved lengthwise, then cut on diagonal into ½-inch-thick slices

Cook carrots in pot of boiling salted water until crisp-tender, about 4 minutes. Drain.

Heat oil in large pot over medium-high heat. Add garlic, tarragon, and thyme; sauté about 30 seconds. Add carrots and remaining vegetables; sauté until just tender, tossing often, about 6 minutes. Sprinkle with salt and pepper.

8 SERVINGS

Roasted Curried Cauliflower

12 cups cauliflower florets (from about 4 pounds cauliflower)

1 large onion, peeled, quartered

1 teaspoon coriander seeds

1 teaspoon cumin seeds

¾ cup olive oil

½ cup red wine vinegar

3½ teaspoons curry powder

1 tablespoon Hungarian hot paprika

1¾ teaspoons salt

¼ cup chopped fresh cilantro

Preheat oven to 450°F. Place cauliflower florets in large roasting pan. Pull apart onion quarters into separate layers; add to cauliflower. Stir coriander seeds and cumin seeds in small skillet over medium heat until slightly darkened, about 5 minutes. Crush coarsely in mortar with pestle. Place seeds in medium bowl. Whisk in oil, vinegar, curry powder, paprika, and salt. Pour dressing over vegetables; toss to coat. Spread vegetables in single layer. Sprinkle with pepper.

Roast vegetables until tender, stirring occasionally, about 35 minutes. *(Can be made 2 hours ahead. Let stand at room temperature. Rewarm in 450°F oven 10 minutes, if desired.)*

Mound vegetables in large bowl. Sprinkle with fresh cilantro. Serve warm or at room temperature.

6 SERVINGS

Saffron Couscous with Peas and Mint

2¾ cups low-salt chicken broth
1 10-ounce package frozen peas
3 tablespoons butter
¼ teaspoon saffron threads, crumbled
2 cups plain couscous (about 10 ounces)
2 green onions, chopped
3 tablespoons chopped fresh mint

Combine broth, peas, butter, and saffron in heavy large saucepan. Bring to boil over high heat, occasionally stirring until butter melts. Mix in couscous. Remove from heat, cover, and let stand until broth is absorbed and couscous is tender, about 12 minutes. Fluff with fork; mix in green onions and mint. Season to taste with salt and pepper. Mound in bowl.

6 SERVINGS

Spiced Winter Squash with Fennel

- 1 1½-pound butternut squash, peeled, halved lengthwise, seeded, halved crosswise, then cut lengthwise into ¾-inch-wide wedges
- 1 fennel bulb, trimmed, cut lengthwise into 1-inch-wide wedges
- 1 large onion, root end left intact, then cut lengthwise into ½-inch-wide wedges
- 3 tablespoons olive oil
- 1 teaspoon ground cumin
- 1 teaspoon ground cinnamon
- 1 teaspoon chili powder
- ½ teaspoon turmeric

Position rack in bottom third of oven and preheat to 450°F. Combine squash, fennel, and onion on heavy large rimmed baking sheet. Add oil and toss to coat. Mix all spices in small bowl to blend. Sprinkle spice mixture over vegetables and toss to coat. Sprinkle with salt and generous amount of pepper. Roast until vegetables are tender and browned, turning once, about 45 minutes. Transfer to shallow dish and serve.

4 SERVINGS

Brussels Sprouts and Chestnuts with Blue Cheese

- 2 tablespoons olive oil
- 2 large shallots, halved lengthwise, sliced crosswise
- 1 pound brussels sprouts, stem end trimmed, halved lengthwise
- 1 7.25- to 7.4-ounce jar steamed chestnuts
- 1 cup low-salt chicken broth
- ⅓ cup whipping cream
- 3 tablespoons chopped fresh chives
- ½ cup crumbled blue cheese

Heat olive oil in large nonstick skillet over medium-high heat. Add shallots and sauté 1 minute. Add brussels sprouts and chestnuts. Sprinkle with salt and pepper; sauté 1 minute. Add broth and bring to boil. Reduce heat, cover, and simmer until brussels sprouts are almost tender, about 5 minutes. Uncover and boil until almost all liquid evaporates, about 4 minutes. Add cream and boil until brussels sprouts and chestnuts are coated with cream, stirring frequently, about 3 minutes. Mix in chives. Season with salt and generous amount of pepper. Transfer to bowl. Sprinkle with cheese and serve.

6 SERVINGS

Grilled Corn on the Cob with Jalapeño-Lime Butter

2 jalapeño chiles
½ cup (1 stick) butter, room temperature
1 garlic clove, minced
1 teaspoon grated lime peel

6 ears fresh corn, unhusked

Prepare barbecue (high heat). Grill chiles until charred on all sides. Cool 5 minutes. Using small paring knife, peel chiles. Scrape out seeds and pale membranes; discard. Coarsely chop chiles; transfer to processor. Add butter, garlic, and lime peel; process until smooth. Season jalapeño-lime butter to taste with salt. Transfer to small bowl. (*Can be made 1 day ahead. Cover and chill. Bring to room temperature before serving.*)

Grill corn until husks are blackened on all sides, turning occasionally, about 15 minutes. Wearing oven mitts to protect hands, remove husks and silk from corn. Serve with jalapeño-lime butter and salt.

6 SERVINGS

Tricolor Vegetable Sauté with Cumin Seeds and Oregano

2 tablespoons olive oil
1 red onion, halved, sliced
1 large red bell pepper, cut into ⅓-inch-wide strips
1 large yellow bell pepper, cut into ⅓-inch-wide strips
1 large poblano chile,* seeded, cut into ⅓-inch-wide strips
1 tablespoon cumin seeds
4 medium zucchini (about 1 pound), trimmed, cut on sharp diagonal into ⅓-inch-thick slices
2 tablespoons chopped fresh oregano

Heat oil in large nonstick skillet over medium-high heat. Add next 5 ingredients; sauté until vegetables are slightly softened, about 5 minutes. Add zucchini and oregano; sauté until zucchini is crisp-tender, about 5 minutes longer. Season with salt and pepper. Cool to room temperature.

A fresh green chile, often called a pasilla; *available at many supermarkets and Latin American markets.*

8 SERVINGS

Celebration Dinner for 6

Caviar and Blini

Champagne

Pepper-Crusted Steaks with Worcestershire Sauce
(*page 52*)

Brussels Sprouts and Chestnuts with Blue Cheese
(*opposite*)

Potato Gratin

Cabernet Sauvignon

Crème Fraîche Cheesecake with Honey-Rum-Roasted Pineapple
(*page 200*)

Cognac and *Coffee*

Salad with Goat Cheese and Drambuie-Poached Pears

PEARS

  1 cup water

  ½ cup Drambuie (Scotch-based liqueur) or brandy

  ¼ cup sugar

  1 teaspoon whole allspice

  4 firm but ripe Anjou or Bosc pears, peeled

SALAD

  ½ cup vegetable oil

  3 tablespoons white wine vinegar

  2 5-ounce bags mixed baby greens

  1 5- to 6-ounce log soft fresh goat cheese, cut into 8 rounds

FOR PEARS: Bring 1 cup water, Drambuie, sugar, and allspice to boil in heavy medium saucepan over high heat, stirring until sugar dissolves. Add pears. Reduce heat to low, cover, and simmer until pears are tender, turning pears twice, about 20 minutes. Remove from heat, uncover, and cool completely, turning pears occasionally in syrup. Cover; chill at least 3 hours and up to 2 days.

Using slotted spoon, transfer pears to work surface. Cut pears lengthwise into quarters. Core and slice pears.

FOR SALAD: Whisk oil and vinegar in large bowl to blend. Season dressing to taste with salt and pepper. Add greens to dressing and toss to coat. Divide greens among 8 plates. Top each salad with 1 round of goat cheese and pear slices.

8 SERVINGS

Black Bean, Jicama, and Grilled Corn Salad

  2   large ears of corn, husked
  5   tablespoons extra-virgin olive oil, divided
  2   15-ounce cans black beans, rinsed, drained
  1   cup ⅓-inch dice peeled jicama
  ½   cup ⅓-inch dice peeled carrots
  ⅓   cup thinly sliced green onions
  ⅓   cup chopped fresh cilantro
  ¼   cup (packed) chopped fresh basil

  3   tablespoons fresh lime juice
  2   tablespoons orange juice
  2½ teaspoons grated lime peel
  ¼   teaspoon ground cumin

Prepare barbecue (medium-high heat). Brush corn with 1 tablespoon olive oil. Grill corn until tender and brown in spots, turning occasionally, about 10 minutes. Cool slightly. Cut off corn kernels; place in large bowl. Add black beans, diced jicama, carrots, green onions, cilantro, and basil.

Whisk lime juice, orange juice, lime peel, cumin, and remaining 4 tablespoons oil in small bowl. Mix dressing into bean salad. Season generously with salt and pepper. (*Can be made 4 hours ahead. Cover; chill. Let stand at room temperature 1 hour before serving.*)

8 SERVINGS

Backyard Barbecue for 6

Chips and Salsa

Cheeseburgers with Charred Green Chiles and Onions
(*page 46*)

Black Bean, Jicama, and Grilled Corn Salad
(*at left*)

Mixed Green Salad

Beer and *Iced Tea*

Rum-Roasted Pineapple with Rum Raisin Ice Cream
(*page 191*)

Mixed Greens with Honey-Lime Dressing

½ cup olive oil
¼ cup fresh lime juice
2 teaspoons honey
1 teaspoon grated lime peel
1 cup paper-thin slices red onion

2 6-ounce bags mixed lettuces
6 plum tomatoes, thinly sliced

Whisk first 4 ingredients in small bowl to blend. Season dressing with salt and pepper. Transfer 2 tablespoons dressing to another small bowl; mix in onion. Let onion and remaining dressing stand at least 1 hour and up to 3 hours. Toss onion mixture occasionally.

Mix lettuces, tomatoes, and onion mixture in bowl. Toss with dressing.

8 SERVINGS

Orzo Salad with Heirloom Tomatoes and Herbs

8 ounces orzo (rice-shaped pasta; about 1¼ cups)

2 tablespoons Sherry wine vinegar
1 tablespoon fresh lemon juice
½ cup extra-virgin olive oil
1¼ pounds assorted heirloom tomatoes, cut into ½-inch pieces
¾ cup chopped green onions
½ cup sliced pitted oil-cured olives
¼ cup thinly sliced fresh basil
¼ cup chopped fresh mint
2 tablespoons chopped fresh Italian parsley

Cook orzo in large pot of boiling salted water until tender but still firm to bite, stirring occasionally. Drain. Rinse under cold water; drain well. Transfer to medium bowl; cool.

Whisk vinegar and lemon juice in small bowl; gradually whisk in oil. Pour dressing over orzo. Mix in remaining ingredients. Season to taste with salt and pepper. (*Can be made 2 hours ahead. Let stand at room temperature. Stir before serving.*)

6 SERVINGS

Green Bean and Radicchio Salad with Roasted Beets and Balsamic Red Onions

  1 large red onion, halved lengthwise, thinly sliced crosswise

¼ cup plus 6 tablespoons balsamic vinegar

  1 bay leaf

  6 large beets (about 2½ pounds)

  1 tablespoon plus ½ cup extra-virgin olive oil

  2 tablespoons water

1½ pounds slender green beans, trimmed, cut in half crosswise

¼ cup chopped shallots

  1 tablespoon minced fresh thyme

  1 large head of radicchio

An overnight pickling tames the red onion.

Place onion, ¼ cup vinegar, and bay leaf in large jar or medium bowl. Add just enough water to cover. Season generously with salt and pepper. Cover and chill overnight. *(Can be prepared 3 days ahead.)*

Preheat oven to 350°F. Place large piece of foil on baking sheet. Place beets in center of foil. Drizzle beets with 1 tablespoon oil and 2 tablespoons water. Top with another piece of foil; crimp edges to seal tightly. Roast beets until tender when pierced with fork, about 1 hour 15 minutes. Cool completely.

Cook beans in large pot of boiling salted water until crisp-tender, about 6 minutes. Rinse under cold water to cool. Drain and pat dry.

Whisk 6 tablespoons balsamic vinegar, ½ cup oil, shallots, and thyme in small bowl to blend. Season dressing with salt and pepper. *(Beets, beans, and dressing can be made 1 day ahead. Cover separately and refrigerate.)*

Peel and cut beets into ¼-inch-thick slices. Arrange large radicchio leaves over very large platter to cover (reserve small leaves for another use). Drain red onions; scatter over radicchio. Arrange beans over onions. Arrange beet slices decoratively over beans. Pour dressing over salad and serve.

16 SERVINGS

Dilled Potato and Pickled Cucumber Salad

6 tablespoons distilled white vinegar

4 teaspoons coarse kosher salt

2 1-pound English hothouse cucumbers, very thinly sliced

½ cup plus 3 tablespoons chopped fresh dill

3¼ pounds Yukon Gold potatoes (about 10 medium), unpeeled
Additional coarse kosher salt

1 cup very thinly sliced white onion

8 radishes, trimmed, thinly sliced

¾ cup mayonnaise

Small radishes with green tops

Stir vinegar and 4 teaspoons coarse salt in small bowl until salt dissolves. Place cucumbers and ½ cup dill in heavy 1-gallon resealable plastic bag. Add vinegar mixture; seal bag. Turn several times to coat. Refrigerate overnight, turning bag occasionally.

Pour cucumber mixture into large sieve set over bowl. Drain at least 1 hour and up to 3 hours. Discard brine.

Cook potatoes in large pot of boiling salted water until tender, about 30 minutes. Drain. Cool potatoes completely. Peel potatoes; quarter lengthwise. Cut crosswise into ½-inch-thick slices. Place potatoes in large bowl; sprinkle generously with coarse salt and pepper. Add drained cucumbers, onion, sliced radishes, and remaining 3 tablespoons dill; toss to blend. Let stand 1 hour. Stir mayonnaise into salad. Season generously with salt and pepper, if desired. *(Can be made 1 day ahead. Cover and chill.)*

Mound salad in bowl; garnish with whole radishes. Serve cold or at room temperature.

8 SERVINGS

Pink Grapefruit, Fennel, and Parmesan Salad

1½ tablespoons Champagne vinegar
½ teaspoon honey
¼ cup extra-virgin olive oil
2 heads of Belgian endive, halved lengthwise, cut lengthwise into thin strips
1 head of butter lettuce, leaves torn
1 cup thinly sliced fresh fennel bulb
3 small pink grapefruits, sectioned
1 ounce Parmesan cheese, shaved with vegetable peeler

Inspired by the classic Sicilian winter salad of blood oranges and fennel.

Whisk vinegar and honey in large bowl to blend. Whisk in olive oil; season dressing to taste with salt and pepper. Add endive, butter lettuce, and fennel to bowl; toss to coat. Top salad with grapefruit sections, then Parmesan cheese, and serve.

6 SERVINGS

Carrot Salad with Orange, Green Olives, and Green Onions

3 pounds carrots, peeled, cut on diagonal into
¼-inch-thick slices

¼ cup extra-virgin olive oil
¼ cup fresh lemon juice
1 tablespoon grated orange peel
1 tablespoon ground coriander
 Drizzle of honey (optional)
1 cup drained chopped pitted brine-cured green olives
1 cup chopped green onions

 Orange slices
 Fresh Italian parsley sprigs

Cook carrots in large pot of boiling salted water until crisp-tender, about 7 minutes. Drain well.

Whisk oil, lemon juice, orange peel, and coriander in large bowl to blend. Add hot carrots and toss to coat. Cool, tossing occasionally. Season with salt and pepper. Drizzle with honey, if desired. Stir in olives and green onions. Cover and refrigerate at least 3 hours. (*Can be made 1 day ahead. Keep refrigerated.*)

Stir salad to redistribute dressing. Garnish edges of platter with orange slices and parsley. Mound carrots in center.

16 SERVINGS

Tomato and Corn Salad with Marjoram

4 ears fresh corn, husked

¼ cup extra-virgin olive oil
1 tablespoon red wine vinegar
3 medium tomatoes, chopped
½ cup crumbled feta cheese
2 tablespoons chopped fresh marjoram

4 large butter lettuce leaves

Cook corn in large pot of boiling salted water until tender, about 5 minutes. Cool. Cut corn kernels from cobs.

Whisk olive oil and vinegar in medium bowl to blend. Add corn, tomatoes, feta cheese, and marjoram; toss to coat.

Arrange lettuce leaves on platter. Spoon tomato and corn salad onto leaves and serve.

4 SERVINGS

Cabbage, Fresh Fennel, and Carrot Slaw

  1 2½-pound cabbage, quartered, cored, very thinly sliced (about 18 cups)
  2 fresh fennel bulbs, trimmed, halved, very thinly sliced (about 3 cups)
  1 small onion, thinly sliced
  1 very large carrot, peeled, coarsely shredded
 ¾ cup mayonnaise
 ½ cup sour cream
  2 tablespoons fresh lemon juice
 ½ teaspoon sugar
 ½ teaspoon hot pepper sauce

Combine cabbage, fennel, onion, and carrot in large bowl. Whisk mayonnaise, sour cream, lemon juice, sugar, and hot sauce in medium bowl to blend. Season dressing to taste with salt and pepper. Add dressing to cabbage mixture; toss to coat. Season slaw to taste with salt and pepper. Refrigerate at least 1 hour and up to 2 hours, tossing occasionally. Transfer to serving bowl.

10 SERVINGS

Bibb Lettuce, Watercress, and Radish Salad

  3 tablespoons white wine vinegar
  1 tablespoon Dijon mustard
  1 tablespoon chopped fresh tarragon
 ½ cup olive oil

  1 large head of Bibb lettuce, coarsely torn (about 9 cups)
  1 large bunch watercress, tough stems trimmed (about 4 cups)
  4 green onions, chopped
  4 large radishes, thinly sliced

Whisk vinegar, mustard, and tarragon in bowl to blend. Whisk in oil. Season with salt and pepper.

Combine lettuce, watercress, green onions, and radishes in large bowl. Toss with enough dressing to coat and serve.

8 SERVINGS

Salad with Teardrop Tomatoes and Parsley Vinaigrette

¾ cup olive oil
¼ cup red wine vinegar
¼ cup freshly grated Parmesan cheese
   (scant 1 ounce)
¼ cup chopped fresh Italian parsley
1½ teaspoons Dijon mustard

8 cups coarsely torn green curly leaf
   lettuce (about ½ large head)
6 cups coarsely torn red leaf lettuce
   (about ½ head)
2 cups arugula (about 2½ ounces)
2 cups red and/or yellow teardrop
   tomatoes, halved

Blend olive oil, red wine vinegar, grated Parmesan cheese, chopped Italian parsley, and Dijon mustard in blender until smooth. Season vinaigrette to taste with salt and pepper. (*Can be made 2 hours ahead. Let stand at room temperature.*)

Combine lettuces, arugula, and tomatoes in large bowl. Toss salad with enough vinaigrette to coat and serve.

6 SERVINGS

Soba Noodle Salad with Cucumber and Mango

¾ cup rice vinegar
¼ cup sugar
¾ teaspoon salt
3 large garlic cloves, chopped
1 red jalapeño or serrano chile, seeded, chopped
3 tablespoons fresh lime juice
1 tablespoon oriental sesame oil
1½ teaspoons grated lime peel

12 ounces green soba or chuka soba (Japanese-style) noodles*

1 large English hothouse cucumber, halved lengthwise, thinly sliced crosswise
1 large ripe mango, peeled, halved, pitted, thinly sliced crosswise
1 cup chopped fresh basil
1 cup chopped fresh mint
1 cup chopped toasted salted peanuts
  Lime wedges

Warm vinegar, sugar, and salt in small saucepan over medium heat, stirring occasionally until sugar dissolves, about 1 minute. Stir in garlic and jalapeño. Cool. Mix in lime juice, sesame oil, and lime peel.

Cook noodles in large pot of boiling salted water until tender but still firm to bite, stirring occasionally. Drain well. Rinse under cold water; drain again. Transfer noodles to dish-towel-lined platter to drain. Transfer noodles to large bowl. Add dressing and toss to coat. *(Can be prepared 6 hours ahead. Cover and refrigerate.)*

Add cucumber, mango, basil, and mint to noodles and toss gently. Arrange salad on platter. Sprinkle with chopped peanuts. Garnish with lime wedges. *(Can be prepared 2 hours ahead. Cover and let stand at room temperature.)*

*Soba noodles are available in the Asian foods section of some supermarkets and at Asian markets.

12 SERVINGS

Danish Potato Salad

   3 pounds medium Yukon Gold potatoes (each about 3 inches in diameter)
  ½ cup finely chopped fresh chives or green onion tops
  ½ cup chopped fresh parsley
  2 tablespoons drained capers
  3 tablespoons white wine vinegar
  1 tablespoon caper liquid from jar
  1 teaspoon coarse-grained Dijon mustard
  ½ cup extra-virgin olive oil

Cook potatoes in large pot of boiling salted water until tender, about 15 minutes. Drain potatoes; cool 30 minutes. Peel potatoes, if desired; cut into ⅓-inch-thick slices. Place potatoes in large bowl. Add chives, parsley, and capers. Combine vinegar, caper liquid, and mustard in small bowl. Whisk in oil. Season dressing to taste with salt and pepper. Pour dressing over potatoes; toss gently. Season salad with salt and pepper. *(Can be made 2 hours ahead. Let stand at room temperature.)*

6 TO 8 SERVINGS

Roasted Pepper Salad with Bacon Dressing and Pine Nuts

4 medium-size red bell peppers
4 medium-size yellow bell peppers

8 bacon slices (about 8 ounces)
2 garlic cloves, minced
¼ teaspoon dried crushed red pepper
2 teaspoons chopped fresh thyme
1 tablespoon Sherry wine vinegar
¼ teaspoon coarse kosher salt
¼ cup pine nuts, toasted

Char peppers over open flame or in broiler until blackened on all sides. Transfer peppers to large bowl; cover tightly with plastic wrap. Let stand 15 minutes. Peel and seed peppers. Cut peppers into ⅓-inch-wide strips; place in medium bowl. *(Can be prepared 6 hours ahead. Cover and let stand at room temperature.)*

Cook bacon in heavy large skillet over medium heat until crisp. Transfer bacon to paper towels to drain. Add garlic and crushed red pepper to drippings in skillet and stir until garlic begins to brown, about 1 minute. Add thyme and stir 10 seconds. Stir in vinegar and ¼ teaspoon salt. Pour warm dressing over peppers in bowl. Crumble bacon and add to peppers along with pine nuts; toss to coat. Season to taste with additional salt and pepper and serve.

8 SERVINGS

Two-Tone Coleslaw with Celery-Seed Yogurt Dressing

½ cup plain low-fat yogurt
⅓ cup light mayonnaise
3 tablespoons apple cider vinegar
2 tablespoons grated onion
1 teaspoon sugar
1 teaspoon celery seeds
3 cups thinly sliced green cabbage
3 cups thinly sliced red cabbage
½ large green bell pepper, thinly sliced into strips
½ cup coarsely grated peeled carrots
2 tablespoons chopped fresh dill, divided

Whisk yogurt, mayonnaise, vinegar, onion, sugar, and celery seeds in large bowl to blend. Add green and red cabbage, bell pepper, carrots, and 1 tablespoon dill. Toss to blend. Season salad to taste with salt and pepper. Cover and refrigerate 1 hour. *(Can be made 2 hours ahead. Keep refrigerated. Toss to blend before using.)* Sprinkle salad with remaining 1 tablespoon dill and serve.

4 SERVINGS

This pretty salad is great alongside grilled sausages, chicken, or burgers.

Artichoke, Fennel, and Edamame Salad

8 tablespoons fresh lemon juice, divided

3 pounds baby artichokes

   Nonstick vegetable oil spray

3 tablespoons plus ½ cup olive oil

¼ cup chopped shallots

1 teaspoon fennel seeds

1 teaspoon grated lemon peel

3 medium fennel bulbs, trimmed (fronds reserved), quartered, thinly
   sliced crosswise (about 4 cups)

½ cup chopped fresh Italian parsley

4½ cups cooked shelled edamame

Sliced raw fennel, roasted baby artichokes, and bright green edamame make one fabulous, Italian-inspired salad.

Preheat oven to 400°F. Fill medium bowl with cold water. Add 2 tablespoons lemon juice. Working with 1 artichoke at a time, pull off tough outer leaves (about 3 rows). Cut tip and stem off artichoke. Cut artichoke in half. Scoop out any choke. Place in lemon water.

Spray large rimmed baking sheet with nonstick spray. Drain artichokes; pat dry. Return to bowl. Add 3 tablespoons oil and toss. Transfer to prepared sheet; sprinkle with salt and pepper. Roast until tender when pierced, stirring once, about 20 minutes. Cool on sheet.

Whisk remaining 6 tablespoons lemon juice, ½ cup oil, shallots, fennel seeds, and lemon peel in large bowl. Stir in sliced fennel, parsley, artichokes, and edamame. Season with salt and pepper. *(Can be made 1 day ahead. Cover and chill.)* Garnish with reserved fennel fronds.

16 SERVINGS

Rosemary-Semolina Round with Sesame and Sea Salt

1¾ cups warm water (105°F to 115°F), divided
1 tablespoon active dry yeast (measured from 2 envelopes)
2¼ cups (about) unbleached all purpose flour, divided

½ cup extra-virgin olive oil
2 teaspoons minced fresh rosemary
2½ cups (or more) semolina flour (pasta flour)*
2 teaspoons fine-grained sea salt

Additional semolina flour
1 tablespoon sesame seeds, divided

1 teaspoon coarse-grained sea salt

Place 1¼ cups warm water in medium bowl; sprinkle yeast over and stir to blend. Let stand 5 minutes to soften. Whisk to dissolve yeast. Add 1¼ cups all purpose flour; whisk until smooth. Cover bowl with plastic wrap. Let stand at room temperature (about 75°F) until bubbles form and yeast mixture has more than doubled in volume, about 45 minutes.

Whisk remaining ½ cup warm water, olive oil, and rosemary in large bowl to blend. Using rubber spatula, mix in semolina flour and 2 teaspoons fine-grained sea salt (dough will be very dry). Stir in yeast mixture. Work in ¾ cup all purpose flour. Turn dough out onto lightly floured surface. Knead until smooth, adding more all purpose flour by tablespoonfuls if sticky. Let rest 5 minutes. Knead until dough springs back when pressed with thumb, about 8 minutes.

Lightly oil large bowl. Transfer dough to bowl; turn to coat. Cover with plastic wrap. Let rise at room temperature until doubled in volume, about 1 hour.

Transfer dough to lightly floured surface. Flatten dough into 18x12-inch rectangle. Starting from 1 long side, roll tightly to form 2½-inch-diameter, 20-inch-long log. With seam side down, shape log into ring, inserting 1 end into second end; smooth seam.

Line baking sheet with parchment paper. Sprinkle sheet with additional semolina flour. Transfer dough ring to prepared sheet, reshaping as necessary to form smooth circle. Sprinkle with 1½ teaspoons sesame seeds, pressing lightly to adhere. Cover loosely with plastic wrap. Let bread rise at room temperature until almost doubled in volume, about 45 minutes.

Preheat oven to 400°F. Remove plastic wrap from bread. Using sharp knife, cut ¼-inch-deep slit all the way around top of loaf. Spray bread lightly with water. Sprinkle with 1½ teaspoons sesame seeds and 1 teaspoon coarse-grained salt. Transfer to oven. Bake bread 15 minutes, spraying lightly with water every 5 minutes. Continue to bake without spraying until bread is golden brown and sounds hollow when tapped on bottom, about 30 minutes longer. Transfer bread to rack and cool completely.

Semolina flour is available in some supermarkets, specialty foods stores, and Italian markets.

MAKES 1 LARGE LOAF

Birthday Dinner for 8

Prosciutto-Wrapped Figs with Gorgonzola and Walnuts
(page 13)

Citrus-Marinated Olives
(halve recipe; page 17)

Seared New York Steaks with Arugula Salad and Saint André Cheese
(page 45)

Sautéed Mushrooms

Rosemary-Semolina Round with Sesame and Sea Salt
(opposite, pictured opposite)

Burgundy

Devil's Food Cake with Chocolate-Orange Buttercream
(page 196)

Chive Popovers

4 large eggs
2 cups whole milk, room temperature
2 cups all purpose flour
¼ cup finely chopped fresh chives
2 tablespoons (¼ stick) unsalted butter, melted
1 teaspoon salt

Preheat oven to 425°F. Butter 20 muffin cups. Mix all ingredients in bowl. Whisk until only tiny specks of flour remain, about 1 minute. *(Can be made 2 hours ahead. Cover; let stand at room temperature.)*

Divide batter among muffin cups. Without opening oven door at any point, bake popovers 15 minutes. Reduce oven temperature to 350°F and continue to bake until puffed, brown, and crisp, about 15 minutes longer. Loosen popovers from pans. Transfer to basket and serve hot.

MAKES 20

Walnut, Golden Raisin, and Fennel Seed Scones

2 cups all purpose flour
⅓ cup sugar
2 teaspoons baking powder
½ teaspoon salt
6 tablespoons chilled unsalted butter, cut into ½-inch cubes
2 large egg yolks
½ cup buttermilk
½ cup golden raisins
⅓ cup chopped toasted walnuts
1 tablespoon fennel seeds
1 large egg beaten to blend with 1 tablespoon water (for glaze)

Preheat oven to 400°F. Butter large baking sheet. Whisk flour, sugar, baking powder, and salt in large bowl to blend. Add butter. Using fingertips, blend mixture until coarse meal forms. Whisk egg yolks and buttermilk in small bowl to blend. Slowly stir egg mixture into flour mixture. Gently stir in raisins, walnuts, and fennel seeds. Turn dough out onto lightly floured work surface and knead gently just until smooth, about 4 turns. Divide dough in half; pat each half into 6-inch round. Cut each round into 6 wedges. Transfer scones to prepared baking sheet. Brush with egg glaze. Bake until scones are light brown, about 17 minutes. Serve warm or at room temperature.

MAKES 12

Skillet Cornbread with Roasted Poblano and Oregano

1 medium poblano chile* (about 3½ ounces)

2 cups yellow cornmeal

1½ cups all purpose flour

½ cup sugar

1½ teaspoons salt

1 teaspoon baking powder

1 teaspoon baking soda

¼ teaspoon ground black pepper

3 large eggs

1 cup whole milk

¼ cup sour cream

1 tablespoon minced fresh oregano

¼ cup (½ stick) unsalted butter

This moist bread is best fresh from the oven, but it can also be made ahead and reheated.

Char poblano chile over open flame or in broiler until blackened on all sides. Enclose in paper bag 15 minutes. Peel, seed, and finely chop chile.

Preheat oven to 350°F. Whisk cornmeal, flour, sugar, salt, baking powder, baking soda, and black pepper in large bowl to blend. Whisk eggs, milk, and sour cream in medium bowl to blend. Mix in poblano chile and oregano. Add egg mixture to dry ingredients and fold in with rubber spatula; do not overmix.

Melt butter in 10-inch-diameter ovenproof skillet with 2-inch-high sides over medium heat, swirling to coat bottom and sides of skillet. Remove from heat. Spread batter evenly in skillet. Bake until cornbread is golden brown around edges and tester inserted into center comes out clean, about 30 minutes. Cool bread 15 minutes in skillet. (*Can be made 6 hours ahead. Cool completely in skillet. Rewarm in 350°F oven 15 minutes.*) Cut bread into wedges and serve warm from skillet.

A fresh green chile, often called a pasilla, *available in some supermarkets and at Latin American markets.*

8 SERVINGS

Cinnamon-Chip and Pecan Loaf

    1   16- to 17-ounce package date-bread mix
   ½   cup (1 stick) plus 2 tablespoons butter, room temperature

    1   cup sour cream
    2   large eggs
   ½   cup cinnamon chips or chocolate chips
   ⅓   cup chopped pecans
    1   teaspoon ground cinnamon
   ½   teaspoon ground allspice

Preheat oven to 350°F. Butter and flour 9x5x2-inch metal loaf pan. Using electric mixer, beat bread mix and ½ cup butter in large bowl until crumbly mixture forms. Transfer ½ cup crumb mixture to small bowl; add remaining 2 tablespoons butter and rub in with fingertips until moist clumps form (for streusel).

Stir sour cream and eggs into remaining crumb mixture in large bowl. Mix in cinnamon chips, pecans, cinnamon, and allspice. Pour batter into prepared pan. Sprinkle with streusel.

Bake until tester inserted into center comes out clean, about 1 hour 20 minutes. Turn out onto rack. Place streusel side up; cool 20 minutes. Serve warm or at room temperature.

10 SERVINGS

Fig Focaccia with Gorgonzola Cheese

    1   10-ounce tube refrigerated pizza dough
   ½   cup finely chopped stemmed dried Calimyrna figs (about 5), divided
    4   canned figs, drained, patted dry, sliced
   ¾   cup crumbled Gorgonzola cheese
    1   tablespoon (packed) dark brown sugar
    1   teaspoon ground black pepper

Preheat oven to 425°F. Roll out dough on work surface to 12x9-inch rectangle. Sprinkle ¼ cup dried figs over center third of dough. Fold left side of dough over figs. Sprinkle with remaining ¼ cup dried figs. Fold right side of dough over second layer of figs to cover. Using rolling pin, gently flatten dough to 12x7-inch rectangle; place on baking sheet. Arrange fig slices atop dough. Sprinkle with Gorgonzola, then sugar and pepper. Bake bread until golden brown and cheese melts, about 25 minutes. Serve bread warm.

4 TO 6 SERVINGS

Ginger-Lime Coconut Cake
with Marshmallow Frosting
(page 202)

Desserts

Pies & Tarts

Fruit Desserts

Cakes

Mousses & Puddings

Frozen Desserts

Cookies

Lemon Crème Brûlée Tart

CRUST

- 1 cup all purpose flour
- ¼ cup powdered sugar
  Pinch of salt
- 6 tablespoons (¾ stick) chilled unsalted butter, cut into ½-inch cubes
- 4 teaspoons (or more) chilled whipping cream
- 1 egg white, beaten to blend

FILLING

- ¾ cup plus 2 tablespoons sugar
- ¾ cup whipping cream
- 4 large egg yolks
- 2 large eggs
- ½ cup fresh lemon juice
- 1 tablespoon (packed) finely grated lemon peel

  Lemon slices (optional)

FOR CRUST: Combine flour, sugar, and salt in processor; blend 5 seconds. Using on/off turns, blend in butter until coarse meal forms. Add 4 teaspoons cream. Using on/off turns, blend until moist clumps form, adding more cream by teaspoonfuls if dough is dry. Gather dough into ball; flatten into disk. Wrap and chill at least 2 hours.

Preheat oven to 350°F. Roll out dough on floured surface to 12-inch round. Transfer to 9-inch-diameter tart pan with removable bottom. Fold overhang in, pressing to form double-thick sides. Bake crust until golden, pressing with back of fork if crust bubbles, about 18 minutes (small cracks may appear). Brush inside of hot crust twice with egg white. Maintain oven temperature.

FOR FILLING: Whisk ¾ cup sugar, cream, yolks, and eggs in bowl to blend well. Mix in lemon juice and lemon peel. Pour filling into warm crust. Bake until filling is slightly puffed at edges and set in center, about 30 minutes. Cool completely, about 1 hour.

Preheat broiler. Place tart on baking sheet. Cover edge of crust with foil to prevent burning. Sprinkle tart with 2 tablespoons sugar. Broil tart until sugar melts and caramelizes, turning sheet for even browning, about 2 minutes. Transfer tart to rack. Cool until topping is crisp, about 1 hour.

Push tart pan bottom up, releasing tart. Place on platter, garnish with lemon slices, if desired, and serve.

8 SERVINGS

Quick Apple Tart

- 1   sheet frozen puff pastry (half of 17.3-ounce package), thawed
- 3   medium Golden Delicious apples, peeled, cored, very thinly sliced
- 2   tablespoons (¼ stick) unsalted butter, melted
- 3   tablespoons cinnamon sugar (or 3 tablespoons sugar mixed with scant ½ teaspoon ground cinnamon)
- ¼   cup apricot jam, melted

Preheat oven to 400°F. Line baking sheet with parchment paper. Unfold pastry on parchment paper. Using tines of fork, pierce ½-inch border around edge of pastry, then pierce center all over. Arrange apples atop pastry in 4 rows, overlapping apple slices and leaving border clear. Brush apples with melted butter; sprinkle with cinnamon sugar. Bake 30 minutes. Brush melted jam over apples. Bake tart until golden, about 8 minutes.

This dessert is as impressive as it is simple. And any number of variations would be equally tempting. Try using a mixture of apples and pears, substituting ground ginger for the cinnamon, or sprinkling the warm tart with finely chopped pecans.

6 SERVINGS

Almond, Apricot, and Cherry Tart

CRUST

1½   cups all purpose flour
⅓   cup whole almonds, toasted
¼   teaspoon salt
½   cup (1 stick) unsalted butter, room temperature
⅓   cup powdered sugar
 1   large egg

FILLING

 2   ounces crumbled almond paste* (about 3 packed tablespoons)
 6   tablespoons sugar, divided
3½   tablespoons unsalted butter, room temperature
 1   large egg
 3   tablespoons cake flour
 9   medium apricots (about 22 ounces), pitted, quartered
20   cherries, pitted, halved

FOR CRUST: Blend first 3 ingredients in processor until almonds are finely ground. Using electric mixer, beat butter and powdered sugar in medium bowl until blended. Beat in egg. Add flour mixture; beat until blended. Gather dough into ball; flatten into square. Wrap in plastic; refrigerate 1 hour.

Roll out dough on floured surface to 10-inch square. Transfer to 9-inch square tart pan with removable bottom; press crust over bottom and up sides of pan. Trim any excess dough. Pierce crust all over with fork; chill at least 2 hours. (*Can be made 1 day ahead. Cover; keep chilled.*)

FOR FILLING: Preheat oven to 350°F. Using electric mixer, beat almond paste and 4 table-spoons sugar in medium bowl until fine meal forms, about 3 minutes. Add butter; beat until almost smooth. Add egg; beat until smooth. Beat in flour. Spread filling evenly in unbaked crust. Arrange apricot quarters on sides with rounded side up in rows atop filling. Place cherry halves between apricots. Sprinkle remaining 2 tablespoons sugar over fruit.

Bake tart 30 minutes. Reduce oven temperature to 325°F. Bake until crust is golden and filling is puffed and golden, about 30 minutes longer. Cool tart in pan on rack at least 1 hour. Serve tart warm or at room temperature.

Available in the baking products section of most supermarkets and in specialty foods stores.

8 SERVINGS

Sweet Potato Tartes Tatins with Pumpkin-Seed Brittle

PUMPKIN-SEED BRITTLE

    Nonstick vegetable oil spray

¼ cup sugar

    Pinch of salt

1 cup raw shelled pumpkin seeds, toasted

TARTES

1 tablespoon plus 1 teaspoon vanilla extract

1 teaspoon salt

2 large 3-inch-diameter yams (red-skinned sweet potatoes), peeled, cut crosswise into eight
     ½-inch-thick slices total

1 cup plus 1 tablespoon sugar

10 tablespoons unsalted butter, cut into 1-inch cubes, room temperature

1 17.3-ounce package frozen puff pastry (2 sheets), thawed

1 large egg

    Vanilla ice cream

FOR PUMPKIN-SEED BRITTLE: Spray large rimmed baking sheet with nonstick spray. Stir sugar, 2 tablespoons water, and pinch of salt in small saucepan over medium heat until sugar dissolves. Increase heat to high. Boil without stirring until mixture turns deep amber, occasionally swirling pan and brushing down sides with wet pastry brush, about 5 minutes. Stir in pumpkin seeds; immediately spread out on baking sheet. Cool until hardened. Break into pieces. *(Can be made 2 days ahead. Store in airtight container at room temperature.)*

FOR TARTES: Bring 8 cups water, 1 tablespoon vanilla, and 1 teaspoon salt to boil in heavy large saucepan. Add yam slices; cook until just tender, about 6 minutes (do not overcook). Using slotted spoon, transfer yam slices to rack; cool.

Preheat oven to 375°F. Lightly spray eight ³/₄-cup ramekins or custard cups with nonstick spray. Stir 1 cup sugar and 3 tablespoons water in heavy small saucepan over medium heat until sugar dissolves. Increase temperature to high. Boil without stirring until syrup turns deep amber, occasionally swirling pan and brushing down sides with wet pastry brush, about 5 minutes. Remove from heat. Gradually add butter, whisking until melted and smooth (mixture will bubble). Whisk in remaining 1 teaspoon vanilla. Divide caramel among ramekins. Place 1 yam slice atop caramel in each ramekin.

Using 3¹/₂-inch round cookie cutter, cut pastry into 8 disks. Pierce pastry all over with fork. Top each yam slice with pastry disk. Beat egg in bowl to blend. Brush pastry lightly with egg. Sprinkle with 1 tablespoon sugar. Bake until pastry is browned and puffed, about 25 minutes.

Invert tartes onto plates. Serve warm with ice cream and brittle.

MAKES 8

Sophisticated Southwestern Dinner for 8

Brie and Grape Quesadillas

Roast New York Strip Loin with Adobo Rub
(page 53)

Sautéed Chayote Squash

Rice

Cabernet Sauvignon

Sweet Potato Tartes Tatins with Pumpkin-Seed Brittle
(opposite, pictured opposite)

Rhubarb and White Chocolate Lattice Tart

CRUST

 2 cups all purpose flour
 3 tablespoons sugar
 ½ teaspoon salt
 10 tablespoons (1¼ sticks) chilled unsalted butter, cubed
 1 large egg
 2 tablespoons (about) chilled whipping cream

FILLING

 5 cups (about 1½ pounds) 1-inch pieces rhubarb
 ⅓ cup sugar
 2 tablespoons whisky

 8 ounces high-quality white chocolate (such as Lindt or Perugina), chopped
 1 tablespoon whipping cream beaten with 2 teaspoons sugar (for glaze)

    Whipped cream

FOR CRUST: Combine flour, sugar, and salt in processor; blend 5 seconds. Add butter. Using on/off turns, process until mixture resembles coarse meal. Whisk egg and 1 tablespoon cream in small bowl to blend; add to flour mixture. Using on/off turns, blend until dough comes together in moist clumps, adding more cream by teaspoonfuls if dough is dry. Gather dough into ball. Shape ⅔ of dough into disk; shape remaining dough into rectangle. Wrap both dough pieces and chill at least 2 hours and up to 1 day.

FOR FILLING: Combine rhubarb, sugar, and whisky in large skillet. Sauté over medium heat until sugar dissolves and syrup begins to bubble. Cover and simmer until rhubarb is almost tender, about 6 minutes. Transfer contents of skillet to strainer set over large bowl (reserve skillet). Drain rhubarb well. Return juices from bowl to same skillet. Boil over medium-high heat until juices are reduced to 3 tablespoons, about 5 minutes. Remove skillet from heat and reserve juices.

Preheat oven to 375°F. Roll out dough rectangle on lightly floured surface to 9½-inch square; cut into 9 strips. Arrange strips on small baking sheet; chill.

Roll out dough disk on lightly floured surface to 11-inch round. Transfer to 9-inch-diameter tart pan with removable bottom. Trim overhang to ¼ inch. Fold in and press sides until top edge of crust is slightly higher than pan side. Pierce crust with fork. Line with foil; fill with dried beans or pie weights. Bake crust until sides are set, about 18 minutes. Remove foil and beans. Bake until crust is pale golden, pressing with back of fork if crust bubbles, about 15 minutes longer. Cool crust 15 minutes.

Sprinkle chopped white chocolate over crust. Top with rhubarb. Spoon rhubarb juices over. Arrange 5 dough strips atop filling, spacing evenly apart. Arrange remaining dough strips atop filling in opposite direction, forming lattice. Seal ends of dough strips to crust,

trimming excess dough. Brush lattice with whipping cream glaze.

Bake tart until filling bubbles and lattice is golden, about 50 minutes. Cool tart slightly in pan on rack. Push up pan bottom, releasing tart. Cut tart into wedges and serve warm or at room temperature with whipped cream.

8 SERVINGS

A touch of whisky enhances the lovely filling.

Black-Bottom Raspberry Cream Pie

CRUST

      Nonstick vegetable oil spray

1¾   cups crushed chocolate wafer cookies (about 30 cookies from one 9-ounce package)

½   cup (1 stick) unsalted butter, melted

¼   cup sugar

FILLING

½   cup sugar

¼   cup unsweetened cocoa powder (preferably Dutch-process)

2   tablespoons cornstarch

2½   cups whole milk, divided

2   large egg yolks

1   large egg

4   ounces bittersweet (not unsweetened) or semisweet chocolate, finely chopped

2   tablespoons (¼ stick) unsalted butter

TOPPING

3   ½-pint containers raspberries

1   cup chilled whipping cream

2   tablespoons powdered sugar

½   teaspoon vanilla extract

The "black bottom" is a layer of superb chocolate pudding—plus a chocolate cookie crust. The pie must be chilled overnight before the topping is added.

FOR CRUST: Spray 9-inch-diameter glass pie dish with nonstick spray. Blend cookie crumbs, butter, and sugar in medium bowl. Press mixture evenly over bottom and up sides (not on rim) of prepared dish. Chill crust 30 minutes.

Preheat oven to 350°F. Bake crust until set, about 10 minutes, then cool.

FOR FILLING: Combine sugar, cocoa, and cornstarch in heavy medium saucepan; whisk to blend well. Gradually add ¼ cup milk, whisking until cornstarch dissolves. Whisk in 2¼ cups milk, then yolks and egg. Stir over medium-high heat until pudding thickens and boils, about 8 minutes. Remove from heat. Add chocolate and butter; whisk until smooth. Spread pudding in crust. Press plastic onto pudding to cover; chill overnight.

FOR TOPPING: Peel plastic wrap off pie. Cover chocolate layer with raspberries, pointed side up, pressing lightly into chocolate to adhere (some berries will be left over). Beat cream, sugar, and vanilla in medium bowl until peaks form; spread over berries on pie. Arrange remaining berries atop cream. Chill pie at least 1 hour and up to 4 hours.

8 TO 10 SERVINGS

Streusel-Topped Apricot Pie with Candied Ginger

CRUST

1¼ cups all purpose flour

1 teaspoon sugar

¼ teaspoon salt

½ cup (1 stick) chilled unsalted butter, cut into ½-inch cubes

3 tablespoons (or more) ice water

TOPPING

½ cup Grape-Nuts cereal

½ cup (packed) golden brown sugar

⅓ cup all purpose flour

⅓ cup toasted slivered almonds, finely chopped

½ teaspoon ground cinnamon

¼ teaspoon ground ginger

¼ teaspoon salt

¼ cup (½ stick) chilled unsalted butter, cut into ½-inch cubes

FILLING

1½ pounds apricots, halved, pitted, cut into ½-inch slices (about 5 cups)

5 tablespoons sugar

3 tablespoons coarsely chopped crystallized ginger

4 teaspoons cornstarch

⅛ teaspoon almond extract

FOR CRUST: Whisk flour, sugar, and salt in large bowl to blend. Add butter; rub in with fingertips until mixture resembles coarse meal. Add 3 tablespoons ice water and stir until moist clumps form, adding more ice water by teaspoonfuls if mixture is too dry. Gather dough into ball; flatten into disk. Wrap in plastic and refrigerate 30 minutes.

Roll out dough on lightly floured surface to 12-inch round. Transfer to 9-inch-diameter pie dish. Fold overhang under and crimp decoratively. Refrigerate 30 minutes.

Preheat oven to 375°F. Line crust with foil; fill with dried beans or pie weights. Bake until dough begins to set, about 20 minutes. Remove foil and beans. Bake until crust is just beginning to brown, about 5 minutes longer. Maintain oven temperature.

MEANWHILE, PREPARE TOPPING: Mix first 7 ingredients in medium bowl to blend. Add butter; rub in with fingertips until moist clumps form.

FOR FILLING: Mix all ingredients in large bowl to blend. Transfer to warm pie crust.

Sprinkle topping over filling. Bake pie until filling is bubbling thickly, about 45 minutes, covering crust with foil after 30 minutes if browning too quickly. Cool.

8 SERVINGS

Coconut Cream Pie with Chocolate Cookie Crust

10 tablespoons (1¼ sticks) unsalted butter, room temperature, divided
1½ cups finely ground chocolate wafer cookies (about 6½ ounces)

1½ cups whole milk
½ cup whipping cream
1 vanilla bean, split lengthwise
1½ cups plus 2 tablespoons sweetened flaked coconut, toasted

6 large egg yolks
½ cup sugar
2 tablespoons cornstarch
Pinch of salt
3 tablespoons coconut rum or dark rum

Sweetened whipped cream

The unusual crust adds a delicious (and striking) twist to this classic dessert.

Preheat oven to 350°F. Melt 6 tablespoons butter in small saucepan. Transfer to medium bowl; mix in cookie crumbs. Press over bottom and up sides of 9-inch-diameter glass pie dish. Bake crust until set, about 10 minutes. Cool.

Mix milk and whipping cream in medium saucepan. Scrape in seeds from vanilla bean; add bean. Bring mixture just to simmer. Remove from heat; cover and let steep 15 minutes. Discard vanilla bean. Mix in 1½ cups toasted coconut. Bring to simmer over medium heat. Remove from heat.

Meanwhile, whisk yolks, sugar, cornstarch, and salt in large bowl to blend. Gradually whisk in hot coconut mixture. Return to same saucepan; bring to boil, stirring constantly. Stir over medium-high heat until thickened, about 30 seconds. Remove from heat. Add 4 tablespoons butter and stir until melted. Stir in rum. Cool filling to lukewarm. Transfer to cooled crust; cover with plastic and chill until cold, at least 4 hours. (*Can be made 1 day ahead. Keep chilled.*)

Pipe or spoon whipped cream over pie, then sprinkle with remaining 2 tablespoons toasted coconut.

8 SERVINGS

Caramelized Pistachio, Walnut, and Almond Tart

CRUST

1¾ cups all purpose flour

⅓ cup powdered sugar

1 teaspoon (scant) salt

⅛ teaspoon ground cloves

10 tablespoons (1¼ sticks) chilled unsalted butter, cut into ½-inch cubes

1 teaspoon grated orange peel

2 tablespoons (or more) ice water

FILLING

1 cup whipping cream (do not use heavy whipping cream)

½ cup sugar

¼ cup (packed) golden brown sugar

¼ cup forest honey or other honey

¾ cup coarsely chopped walnuts, toasted (scant 4 ounces)

¾ cup sliced almonds, toasted (about 3 ounces)

¾ cup shelled unsalted natural pistachios, toasted (scant 4 ounces)

1½ teaspoons rose water*

This candy-like tart with hints of rose, orange, and cloves was inspired by the delicate flavor of baklava. Serve it on its own or with honey-sweetened strained plain yogurt.

FOR CRUST: Blend flour, powdered sugar, salt, and ground cloves in processor. Add butter and orange peel. Using on/off turns, process until mixture resembles coarse meal. Add 2 tablespoons ice water and process until moist clumps form, adding more ice water by teaspoonfuls if mixture is dry. Transfer dough to 10- to 10½-inch tart pan with removable bottom. Press dough evenly onto bottom and up sides of pan. Freeze crust 25 minutes.

MEANWHILE, PREPARE FILLING: Preheat oven to 350°F. Combine cream, both sugars, and honey in heavy medium saucepan. Bring to boil, stirring until sugar dissolves. Continue to boil until mixture darkens and thickens slightly, about 4 minutes. Remove from heat. Stir in all nuts and rose water. Spoon filling evenly into crust.

Bake tart until filling is caramel brown and bubbling thickly and crust is golden, about 38 minutes. Transfer tart to rack and cool completely in pan. Carefully remove pan sides from tart. Place tart on platter. *(Can be prepared 3 days ahead. Cover and store at room temperature.)* Cut tart into wedges and serve at room temperature.

Available at some supermarkets, specialty foods stores, and Middle Eastern markets.

10 TO 12 SERVINGS

Almond and Mixed-Berry Shortcakes

 1 large egg, separated
 5 tablespoons plus ½ cup sugar, divided
 ½ cup sliced almonds

 ½ 7-ounce log almond paste,* cut into ½-inch cubes
 2 cups all purpose flour
 1 tablespoon baking powder
 1 teaspoon grated lemon peel
 ½ teaspoon salt
 ½ teaspoon ground ginger
 6 tablespoons (¾ stick) chilled unsalted butter, cut into ½-inch cubes
 ⅔ cup chilled buttermilk
 1 teaspoon vanilla extract

 2 cups halved hulled strawberries
 1 ½-pint container blackberries
 1 ½-pint container blueberries
 1 ½-pint container raspberries
 1 teaspoon fresh lemon juice
 ¾ cup red currant preserves

    Lightly sweetened whipped cream

Position rack just above center of oven and preheat to 375°F. Line rimmed baking sheet with parchment. Whisk egg white and 3 tablespoons sugar in small bowl to blend. Mix in almonds.

Blend ½ cup sugar and almond paste in processor until fine meal forms. Add flour, baking powder, lemon peel, salt, and ginger; blend 5 seconds. Add butter and cut in, using on/off turns, until coarse meal forms; transfer to large bowl. Whisk egg yolk, buttermilk, and vanilla in small bowl. Gradually add buttermilk mixture to dry ingredients, tossing until moist clumps form. Using floured hands, gather dough together.

Divide dough into 8 equal pieces; roll each into 2-inch ball. Place balls on prepared baking sheet, spacing 2 to 3 inches apart. Gently press top of each ball to flatten slightly. Divide almond topping (including egg white) among biscuits; spread to cover. Bake biscuits until golden brown and tester inserted into centers comes out clean, about 26 minutes (biscuits will spread). Cool on sheet 5 minutes. Transfer to rack and cool. (*Can be made 8 hours ahead. Cover; store at room temperature.*)

Combine berries, lemon juice, and remaining 2 tablespoons sugar in medium bowl. Stir in preserves. Let stand until juices form, at least 1 hour and up to 2 hours, stirring occasionally.

Cut biscuits horizontally in half. Place bottoms on plates. Top with berry mixture, whipped cream, and biscuit tops.

Available in the baking products section of most supermarkets and in specialty foods stores.

MAKES 8

FRUIT
DESSERTS

Pears Poached in Earl Grey Tea with Dried Fruit

        2 cups water
        2 Earl Grey tea bags
     ½ cup sugar
        2 large firm but ripe Bosc pears (about 12 ounces), peeled, halved lengthwise, cored
        8 dried apricot halves
        4 whole cloves
     ¼ cup dried tart cherries*

Bring 2 cups water to boil in medium saucepan. Add tea bags. Remove from heat. Cover and let steep 10 minutes. Discard tea bags. Add sugar to tea and stir over medium heat until dissolved. Add pears, apricots, and cloves. Cover and simmer until pears are just tender, about 5 minutes. Add cherries and simmer 1 minute. Using slotted spoon, transfer pears, apricots, and cherries to bowl. Boil syrup in saucepan until reduced to ³/₄ cup, about 5 minutes. Pour syrup over fruit. Chill until cold, about 3 hours. (*Can be made 1 day ahead. Cover and keep chilled.*)

   Divide fruit and syrup among 4 bowls and serve.

Available in some supermarkets, specialty foods stores, and natural foods stores.

4 SERVINGS

Grapefruit, Ginger, and Star Anise Compote

        1 cup water
        1 cup sugar
     ¼ cup thinly sliced fresh ginger
        6 whole star anise*
     ½ tablespoon grated grapefruit peel

        3 medium-size pink grapefruits, sectioned
        3 medium-size white grapefruits, sectioned

Bring 1 cup water, sugar, ginger, and star anise to boil in medium saucepan over high heat, stirring until sugar dissolves. Reduce heat to medium; simmer until mixture begins to thicken, about 10 minutes. Stir in grapefruit peel. Reduce heat to low; simmer 30 minutes.

   Place all grapefruit sections in large bowl. Using slotted spoon, remove ginger from syrup and discard. Pour hot syrup with star anise over grapefruit; let stand at room temperature 1 hour, stirring occasionally. (*Can be made 4 hours ahead; cover and chill.*) Divide fruit and syrup among 6 small bowls; discard star anise. Serve compote chilled or at room temperature.

Brown star-shaped seedpods, sold in the spice section of some supermarkets and at Asian markets and specialty foods stores.

6 SERVINGS

Plum Cobbler with Cinnamon Biscuits

FILLING

- 4 pounds plums (about 12 large), halved, pitted, cut into ½-inch slices
- 1 cup sugar
- 2½ tablespoons cornstarch
- 1 teaspoon vanilla extract

BISCUITS

- 2 cups all purpose flour
- 5 tablespoons sugar, divided
- 1 tablespoon baking powder
- ½ teaspoon salt
- ½ teaspoon ground cinnamon, divided
- ½ cup (1 stick) chilled unsalted butter, cut into ½-inch cubes
- ¾ cup plus 2 tablespoons whipping cream
- 1 large egg

  Vanilla ice cream

FOR FILLING: Preheat oven to 400°F. Toss plums, sugar, cornstarch, and vanilla in large bowl to coat. Transfer to 13x9x2-inch glass baking dish. Bake until thick and bubbling at edges, about 30 minutes.

MEANWHILE, PREPARE BISCUITS: Whisk flour, 3 tablespoons sugar, baking powder, salt, and ¼ teaspoon cinnamon in large bowl to blend. Add butter; rub in with fingertips until coarse meal forms. Whisk ¾ cup whipping cream and egg in small bowl to blend. Stir cream mixture into flour mixture just until blended. Gently knead in bowl until dough comes together, about 5 turns.

Remove plums from oven and stir gently. Break off golf-ball-size pieces of dough and arrange over hot plums, spacing apart. Brush dough with remaining 2 tablespoons cream. Mix remaining 2 tablespoons sugar and ¼ teaspoon cinnamon in small bowl. Sprinkle over dough.

Bake cobbler until fruit is bubbling, biscuits are browned, and tester inserted into center of biscuits comes out clean, about 30 minutes. Cool slightly. Serve hot or warm with vanilla ice cream.

8 SERVINGS

Fresh Oranges with Spiced Red Wine Syrup

1 750-ml bottle dry red wine
1 cup plus 1 tablespoon sugar
1 cinnamon stick, broken in half

8 oranges

Bring wine, 1 cup sugar, and cinnamon to boil in large saucepan, stirring until sugar dissolves. Boil until reduced to 1 cup, about 18 minutes. Cool syrup completely. Cover and chill until cold. *(Can be made 1 day ahead. Keep chilled.)*

Finely grate peel from 2 oranges. Mix peel and 1 tablespoon sugar in small bowl. Using small sharp knife, cut off peel and white pith from all oranges. Working over large bowl, cut between membranes to release segments. *(Can be made 1 day ahead. Cover orange segments and sugared peel separately and chill.)* Divide oranges and juice among 8 bowls. Drizzle syrup over and sprinkle with sugared orange peel.

8 SERVINGS

Rum-Roasted Pineapple with Rum Raisin Ice Cream

Lunch on the Terrace for 8

Yellow Squash and Mozzarella Quiche with Fresh Thyme
(double recipe; page 120)

Mixed Green Salad

Iced Tea

Fresh Oranges with Spiced Red Wine Syrup
(opposite, pictured opposite)

Butter Cookies

 6 tablespoons (¾ stick) unsalted butter
 1 cup (packed) golden brown sugar
 ½ cup dark rum
 6 whole allspice
 1 vanilla bean, split lengthwise

 8 ¾-inch-thick rounds peeled very ripe pineapple (from 1 large)

 ⅓ cup golden raisins (about 1½ ounces)
 2 pints rum raisin ice cream

Melt butter in heavy medium skillet over medium heat. Whisk in sugar, rum, and allspice. Scrape in seeds from vanilla bean; add bean. Cook until sauce is thick enough to coat spoon and reduced to 1 cup, whisking often, about 10 minutes. Remove from heat; discard vanilla bean and allspice. *(Can be made 1 day ahead. Cover; chill. Rewarm before using.)*

Preheat broiler. Arrange pineapple rounds on rimmed baking sheet. Brush both sides of rounds with some of rum sauce; reserve remaining sauce. Broil pineapple close to heat source until deep brown on top, watching carefully and rotating baking sheet to prevent burning, about 8 minutes. Transfer 1 pineapple round to each of 8 plates.

Add raisins to remaining sauce. Simmer over medium-low heat 3 minutes to blend flavors. Top each pineapple round with scoop of ice cream. Spoon sauce over and serve.

8 SERVINGS

Strawberries in Red Wine Syrup with Crème Fraîche

8   cups halved hulled strawberries (about 2 pounds)
⅓   cup sugar
½   cup dry red wine

2   8-ounce containers (about) crème fraîche or sour cream
    Fresh mint sprigs

Combine berries and sugar in large bowl; toss to coat evenly. Mix in wine. Let stand until sugar dissolves and syrup forms, tossing occasionally, at least 1 hour and up to 2 hours.

Using slotted spoon, divide berries among stemmed dessert goblets. Top with crème fraîche. Spoon syrup over. Garnish with mint sprigs.

8 SERVINGS

Blueberry-Nectarine Crisp

TOPPING

1½ cups all purpose flour

¾ cup (packed) golden brown sugar

½ cup (1 stick) chilled unsalted butter, cut into ½-inch cubes

FILLING

2 pounds large nectarines (about 6), halved, pitted, each half cut into 4 wedges

4 cups fresh blueberries

1 cup ruby Port, divided

2 tablespoons cornstarch

1 teaspoon vanilla extract

½ cup sugar

Vanilla ice cream

Ruby Port in the juicy filling deepens the fruit flavors in this crisp. Top with vanilla ice cream.

FOR TOPPING: Combine flour and brown sugar in medium bowl; whisk to blend. Add butter and rub in with fingertips until small moist clumps form.

FOR FILLING: Preheat oven to 375°F. Butter 13x9x2-inch glass baking dish. Mix nectarines and blueberries in large bowl. Stir ¼ cup Port, cornstarch, and vanilla in small cup until cornstarch dissolves. Combine remaining ¾ cup Port and sugar in heavy medium saucepan. Stir over medium heat until sugar dissolves and mixture comes to boil; continue to boil 3 minutes, whisking occasionally. Whisk in cornstarch mixture and stir until thick and clear, about 30 seconds. Gently stir Port mixture into fruit.

Transfer filling to prepared baking dish. Sprinkle topping evenly over. Bake crisp until nectarines are tender, filling bubbles thickly, and topping is crisp and brown, about 40 minutes. Cool 15 minutes. Serve warm with vanilla ice cream.

8 SERVINGS

Crepes with Caramelized Apples, Rum Sauce, and Vanilla Ice Cream

CREPES

- 3 large eggs
- 1 cup whole milk
- 2 tablespoons dark rum
- 2 tablespoons (¼ stick) unsalted butter, melted
- 1 tablespoon sugar
- ½ teaspoon salt
- ½ teaspoon ground cinnamon
- 1 cup all purpose flour

   Additional melted butter

APPLES

- 5 tablespoons unsalted butter
- 3 pounds medium Golden Delicious apples, peeled, quartered, cored, each quarter cut into 3 wedges
- ¾ cup (packed) golden brown sugar
- ½ cup apple juice
- 2 tablespoons fresh lemon juice
- 1 teaspoon grated lemon peel
- 1 teaspoon ground cinnamon

- 3 tablespoons dark rum

    Vanilla ice cream

There's enough batter to make more than 12 crepes, so don't worry if some aren't perfect.

FOR CREPES: Mix first 7 ingredients in blender until smooth. Add flour in 3 additions, blending until smooth after each addition and scraping down sides of container. Let batter stand at room temperature at least 1 hour and up to 2 hours.

Heat medium nonstick skillet with 7-inch-diameter bottom over medium-high heat. Brush with melted butter. Pour in 3 tablespoonfuls crepe batter, rotating and shaking pan so batter covers bottom evenly. Cook crepe until golden on bottom, about 45 seconds. Turn crepe over and cook until brown in spots, about 30 seconds. Turn crepe out onto paper towel, spotted side up. Repeat with remaining batter, brushing pan with butter before making each crepe and layering each between paper towels. (*Can be made 1 day ahead. Place stack of crepes in very large plastic bag and refrigerate.*)

FOR APPLES: Melt butter in large skillet over high heat. Add apples; sauté until deep golden and tender, tossing often, about 15 minutes. Add sugar, apple juice, lemon juice, lemon peel, and cinnamon. Simmer until juices thicken and apples are very tender, turning with spatula, about 3 minutes. Remove from heat.

Butter large ovenproof rimmed platter. Arrange 12 crepes on work surface, spotted side up. Spoon apples into center of crepes, dividing equally and leaving sauce in skillet. Fold 1 side of crepes over filling; roll up, enclosing filling. Arrange on platter, seam side down. Stir rum into sauce in skillet. Bring to boil, stirring. (*Can be made 3 hours ahead. Let crepes and sauce stand separately at room temperature.*)

Preheat oven to 350°F. Spoon sauce over crepes. Bake until warm, about 10 minutes. Serve with vanilla ice cream.

8 SERVINGS

Devil's Food Cake with Chocolate-Orange Buttercream

CAKE

4 ounces bittersweet (not unsweetened) or semisweet chocolate, chopped

1½ cups all purpose flour
½ cup unsweetened cocoa powder
1 teaspoon baking powder
½ teaspoon coarse kosher salt
¼ teaspoon baking soda
½ cup whole milk
½ cup plain whole-milk yogurt
1½ cups (packed) golden brown sugar
¾ cup (1½ sticks) unsalted butter, room temperature
2 teaspoons dried lavender blossoms,* finely ground in spice mill
4 large eggs

BUTTERCREAM FROSTING

8 ounces bittersweet or semisweet chocolate, chopped
½ cup unsweetened cocoa powder
7 tablespoons (or more) water

1½ cups (3 sticks) unsalted butter, room temperature
4 cups powdered sugar, divided
1 tablespoon grated orange peel
2 teaspoons vanilla extract
½ teaspoon coarse kosher salt
1 tablespoon Grand Marnier or other orange liqueur

Chocolate curls

FOR CAKE: Position rack in center of oven and preheat to 325°F. Butter and flour two 9-inch-diameter cake pans with 1½-inch-high sides. Line bottoms of pans with parchment paper rounds. Stir chocolate in top of double boiler set over simmering water until smooth. Remove from over water. Cool to barely lukewarm.

Sift flour and next 4 ingredients into medium bowl. Whisk milk and yogurt to blend in small bowl. Using electric mixer, beat brown sugar, butter, and lavender in large bowl until smooth. Beat in eggs, 1 at a time. Beat in melted chocolate until smooth. Mix in dry ingredients alternately with milk mixture in 3 additions each. Divide batter between prepared pans.

Bake until tester inserted into centers comes out clean, about 30 minutes. Cool cakes in pans on racks 15 minutes. Turn out onto racks; remove parchment and cool completely.

FOR BUTTERCREAM FROSTING: Stir 8 ounces chocolate in top of double boiler set over simmering water until smooth. Cool until barely lukewarm but still pourable. Mix cocoa powder and 7 tablespoons water in heavy small saucepan. Stir over medium-low heat until smooth and thick but still pourable, adding more water by teaspoonfuls if necessary. Cool.

Beat butter, $^1/_3$ cup powdered sugar, and orange peel in large bowl to blend. Add melted chocolate, vanilla, and salt; beat until smooth. Beat in cocoa mixture. Gradually add remaining $3^2/_3$ cups powdered sugar and beat until frosting is smooth. Mix in Grand Marnier.

Place 1 cake layer on platter. Spread $1^1/_2$ cups frosting over top of cake. Top with second cake layer. Spread remaining frosting over top and sides of cake, swirling decoratively. Mound chocolate curls in center of cake. (*Can be made 1 day ahead. Cover with cake dome and refrigerate. Let cake stand at room temperature 2 hours before serving.*)

Dried lavender blossoms are available at natural foods stores and at some specialty foods stores and farmers' markets.

12 SERVINGS

A subtle hint of lavender accents this lovely dessert. It can also be omitted if you prefer a more traditionally flavored cake.

Lemon-Pistachio Crunch Cake

CURD

8 large egg yolks
¾ cup sugar
½ cup fresh lemon juice
½ cup (1 stick) unsalted butter, cut into ½-inch cubes
2 tablespoons (packed) grated lemon peel
⅛ teaspoon salt

PISTACHIO CRUNCH

⅔ cup sugar
¼ cup (½ stick) unsalted butter
¼ cup water
½ teaspoon baking soda
1 cup natural unsalted pistachios (about 5 ounces)

FROSTING

2½ cups chilled whipping cream, divided
8 ounces high-quality white chocolate (such as Lindt or Perugina), chopped
⅛ teaspoon salt

CAKE

3½ cups cake flour
4 teaspoons baking powder
¾ teaspoon salt
1¼ cups (2½ sticks) unsalted butter, room temperature
2 cups sugar, divided
1 tablespoon vanilla extract
2 teaspoons grated lemon peel
1½ cups whole milk
8 large egg whites

FOR CURD: Whisk all ingredients in heavy medium saucepan to blend. Cook over medium-low heat until curd thickens and candy thermometer registers 170°F, stirring constantly, about 7 minutes (do not boil). Pour curd into small bowl. Press plastic wrap onto surface. Chill at least 1 day and up to 3 days.

FOR PISTACHIO CRUNCH: Place large sheet of foil on work surface; butter foil. Combine sugar, butter, and ¼ cup water in heavy medium saucepan. Stir over medium-low heat until sugar dissolves and butter melts, occasionally brushing down sides of pan with wet pastry brush. Increase heat to medium-high and boil until syrup is medium amber color, stirring constantly, about 12 minutes. Remove from heat. Immediately add baking soda (mixture will foam up), then nuts and stir to blend well. Spread nut mixture onto prepared foil, separating nuts. Cool completely. Chop crunch into ¼- to ⅓-inch pieces. (*Can be made 2 days ahead. Store airtight at room temperature.*)

FOR FROSTING: Bring ³⁄₄ cup cream to simmer in heavy medium saucepan. Remove from heat. Add chocolate and salt; stir until smooth. Transfer frosting base to bowl. Cover; chill overnight.

FOR CAKE: Preheat oven to 350°F. Butter and flour three 9-inch-diameter cake pans with 1¹⁄₂-inch-high sides. Sift flour, baking powder, and salt into medium bowl. Using electric mixer, beat butter in large bowl until fluffy. Gradually add 1³⁄₄ cups sugar, beating until well blended. Beat in vanilla and lemon peel. Beat in flour mixture alternately with milk in 3 additions each. Using clean dry beaters, beat egg whites in another large bowl until soft peaks form. Gradually add remaining ¹⁄₄ cup sugar, beating until stiff but not dry. Fold whites into batter in 3 additions. Divide batter among prepared pans.

Bake cakes until golden and tester inserted into centers comes out clean, about 30 minutes. Cool cakes in pans on racks 15 minutes. Cut around pan sides and turn cakes out onto racks. Turn cakes right side up and cool completely. *(Can be made 1 day ahead. Wrap in foil and store at room temperature.)*

Using serrated knife, cut off mounded tops of cake layers to level. Place 1 cake layer on platter, trimmed side up. Spread with half of lemon curd. Top with second cake layer, trimmed side up. Spread with remaining lemon curd. Top with third cake layer, trimmed side down.

Whisk remaining 1³⁄₄ cups chilled cream into frosting base to loosen. Using electric mixer, beat until frosting holds stiff peaks. Spread over top and sides of cake. Chill until frosting is firm, at least 3 hours. *(Can be made 1 day ahead. Cover with cake dome; keep chilled.)*

Press crunch lightly into frosting on sides and top edge of cake. *(Can be made 1 hour ahead and chilled.)*

12 SERVINGS

A fine-crumbed, very-special-occasion cake. Get started at least one day ahead: The frosting base and lemon curd must chill overnight before using. For the frosting, high-quality white chocolate (such as Lindt or Perugina) works best.

Crème Fraîche Cheesecake
with Honey-Rum-Roasted Pineapple

CRUST

1 cup graham cracker crumbs

¼ cup unsalted butter, melted

1 tablespoon sugar

FILLING

3 8-ounce packages cream cheese, room temperature

1 cup sugar

1 vanilla bean, split lengthwise

2 large eggs

¾ cup crème fraîche or sour cream

TOPPING

1 extra-sweet pineapple, peeled, cut into ½-inch-thick rounds, cored

1 cup water

¼ cup honey

2 tablespoons sugar

2 tablespoons dark rum

FOR CRUST: Preheat oven to 350°F. Blend all ingredients in bowl. Press mixture over bottom of 9-inch-diameter springform pan with 2¾-inch sides. Bake until golden, about 12 minutes. Transfer to rack; cool. Wrap outside of pan with 2 layers of foil. Reduce oven temperature to 325°F.

FOR FILLING: Using electric mixer, beat cream cheese in large bowl until fluffy. Gradually beat in sugar. Scrape in seeds from vanilla bean and blend 1 minute. Beat in eggs 1 at a time. Mix in crème fraîche. Transfer filling to crust. Place cheesecake in roasting pan. Add enough hot water to roasting pan to come 1 inch up sides of springform pan.

Bake cake until top is dry-looking and slightly puffed, about 1 hour. Turn off oven. Let cake cool in closed oven 1 hour. Remove from water bath. Refrigerate uncovered until cold, at least 6 hours. *(Can be made 1 day ahead. Cover and keep refrigerated.)*

FOR TOPPING: Preheat oven to 400°F. Place pineapple rings on large rimmed baking sheet. Boil remaining ingredients in small saucepan 3 minutes, stirring occasionally. Pour syrup over pineapple. Roast pineapple 12 minutes. Turn rings over; roast until tender and syrup thickens, turning rings every 5 minutes, about 20 minutes longer. Cool pineapple on sheet. Cut into ⅓-inch cubes; transfer pineapple and syrup to bowl. *(Can be made 1 day ahead. Chill.)*

Drain pineapple, reserving syrup. Cover top of cheesecake with some pineapple; stir remainder back into syrup. Serve cake, passing remaining pineapple in syrup separately.

12 SERVINGS

Ginger-Lime Coconut Cake
with Marshmallow Frosting

GINGER-LIME CURD

- 3 large eggs
- 3 large egg yolks
- ½ cup sugar
- ½ cup fresh lime juice
- ¼ cup grated lime peel (from about 12 limes)
- 1 tablespoon grated peeled fresh ginger
  Pinch of salt
- 6 tablespoons (¾ stick) unsalted butter, cut into pieces, room temperature

CAKE

- 5 cups sifted cake flour (sifted, then measured)
- 1 teaspoon baking soda
- 1 teaspoon salt
- 1½ cups (3 sticks) unsalted butter, room temperature
- 3 cups sugar
- 8 large eggs
- 2 cups buttermilk, room temperature

  Bamboo skewers

FROSTING

- 1½ cups sugar
- 2 large egg whites
- ⅓ cup water
- 2 teaspoons light corn syrup
- ¼ teaspoon cream of tartar
- 1 teaspoon vanilla extract

- 1 7-ounce package sweetened flaked coconut (about 3 cups)

FOR GINGER-LIME CURD: Whisk eggs, yolks, sugar, lime juice, lime peel, ginger, and salt in large metal bowl to blend. Place bowl over saucepan of barely simmering water (do not allow bottom of bowl to touch simmering water); whisk constantly until curd thickens, about 8 minutes. Remove bowl from over simmering water; whisk butter into curd. Strain through fine strainer set over bowl; discard solids in strainer. Press plastic wrap directly onto surface of curd; chill overnight. (*Curd can be made up to 2 days ahead. Keep refrigerated.*)

FOR CAKE: Position 1 rack in top third and 1 rack in bottom third of oven and preheat oven to 350°F. Butter four 9-inch-diameter cake pans with 1½-inch-high sides. Line bottoms of pans with parchment paper rounds. Butter parchment; dust with flour. Sift flour, baking soda, and salt into large bowl. Using electric mixer, beat butter in another large bowl until smooth. Gradually add sugar and beat until very well blended, about 5 minutes. Beat in eggs 1 at a time, scraping down sides of bowl before each addition. Beat in flour mixture in 3 additions alternately with buttermilk in 2 additions. Divide batter equally among prepared cake pans.

Place 2 cake pans on top rack of oven and 2 pans on bottom rack; bake until golden and tester inserted into cake centers comes out clean, reversing pans after 15 minutes, about 30 minutes total. Cool cakes in pans on racks 10 minutes. Turn cakes out onto racks; peel off parchment paper. Turn cakes right side up on racks; cool completely.

Place 1 cake layer on platter. Spread ⅓ of ginger-lime curd (about ½ cup) over, leaving ½-inch plain border around edge of cake. Repeat procedure on 2 more cake layers. Let each cake layer stand 10 minutes. Stack cake layers, curd side up. Top with fourth cake layer. Let cake stand at room temperature while preparing frosting. Insert 3 or 4 bamboo skewers from top to bottom into cake to hold stacked cake layers in place while frosting.

FOR FROSTING: Whisk sugar, egg whites, ⅓ cup water, light corn syrup, and cream of tartar in large metal bowl to blend. Set bowl over saucepan of barely simmering water (do not allow bottom of bowl to touch simmering water). Using handheld electric mixer, beat on medium speed until mixture resembles soft marshmallow fluff, about 4 minutes. Increase mixer speed to high and beat until mixture is very thick, about 3 minutes longer. Remove bowl from over simmering water. Add vanilla extract and continue beating until marshmallow frosting is completely cool, about 5 minutes longer.

Spread marshmallow frosting thinly over top and sides of cake. Remove bamboo skewers. Press flaked coconut into marshmallow frosting on top and sides of cake. (*Cake can be prepared 1 day ahead. Cover with cake dome and refrigerate. Let stand at room temperature 2 hours before serving.*)

10 TO 12 SERVINGS

This buttermilk layer cake is filled with ginger-scented lime curd, then finished with a sweet and fluffy frosting. Make the lime curd one to two days before assembling the cake.

Chocolate-Amaretti Tortes

TORTES

- 4 ounces semisweet chocolate, chopped
- ¾ cup sliced almonds, toasted
- 12 1½-inch-diameter amaretti cookies* (Italian macaroons), about 2.6 ounces total
- ¼ teaspoon cinnamon
  Pinch of salt
- ½ cup (1 stick) unsalted butter, room temperature
- ½ cup sugar
- 3 large eggs

TOPPING

- ¾ cup chilled whipping cream
- 1½ teaspoons powdered sugar
- ½ teaspoon almond extract

- 2 amaretti cookies, crumbled

FOR TORTES: Position rack in center of oven and preheat to 350°F. Butter four ¾-cup custard cups or soufflé dishes. Dust with flour; tap out excess. Line bottom of cups with parchment paper rounds. Place on rimmed baking sheet.

Stir chocolate in top of double boiler set over simmering water until melted and smooth. Using on/off turns, blend almonds, amaretti, cinnamon, and salt in processor until finely ground. Transfer to medium bowl. Add butter, sugar, and eggs to processor; mix until blended and smooth, occasionally scraping down sides of bowl, about 3 minutes. Add cookie mixture and melted chocolate. Using on/off turns, process just until blended.

Divide batter among custard cups. Bake until tops of tortes are dry and puffed and tester inserted into centers comes out with moist crumbs attached, about 30 minutes. Transfer cups to rack; cool 15 minutes. Run small knife around edges of cups to release tortes. Turn tortes out onto rack and turn right side up; cool. (*Can be made 3 days ahead. Wrap in plastic and store at room temperature.*)

FOR TOPPING: Beat together cream, sugar, and almond extract in medium bowl until cream holds peaks. (*Can be made 4 hours ahead; refrigerate.*)

Place 1 torte on each of 4 plates. Top with dollop of whipped cream, sprinkle with crumbled amaretti, and serve.

Available at some supermarkets and Italian markets.

MAKES 4

Lemon Pound Cake with Berries and Whipped Cream

         3 cups sifted all purpose flour (sifted, then measured)
         1 tablespoon baking powder
       ¾ teaspoon salt
    3⅓ cups sugar, divided
         1 cup (2 sticks) unsalted butter, room temperature
       ½ cup solid vegetable shortening, room temperature
         5 large eggs
         1 cup whole milk
         6 tablespoons fresh lemon juice
         2 tablespoons grated lemon peel

         4 cups halved hulled strawberries
         2 ½-pint containers fresh blackberries

            Whipped cream

This recipe makes two cakes, so freeze one to enjoy at another time.

Preheat oven to 325°F. Butter and flour two 9x5x2¾-inch metal loaf pans. Line pan bottoms with waxed paper. Sift flour, baking powder, and salt into medium bowl. Using electric mixer, beat 3 cups sugar, butter, and shortening in large bowl until well blended. Add eggs 1 at a time, beating to blend after each. Beat in dry ingredients in 3 additions alternately with milk in 2 additions. Beat in lemon juice and lemon peel. Divide batter between prepared pans.

Bake cakes until tester inserted into centers comes out clean, about 55 minutes. Cool cakes in pans 15 minutes. Turn cakes out onto racks; peel off paper. Cool completely.

Combine strawberries, blackberries, and remaining ⅓ cup sugar in small bowl and toss gently to blend. Let stand until juices form, at least 30 minutes and up to 2 hours.

Cut 1 cake crosswise into slices. Serve with berries and whipped cream.

8 TO 10 SERVINGS

Chai-Spiced Honey Bundt Cakes

2½ cups all purpose flour
1½ cups (packed) golden brown sugar
2 teaspoons baking soda
½ teaspoon salt
1¾ cups hot water
1 cup instant chai tea powder*
½ cup honey
½ cup (1 stick) unsalted butter, melted
½ cup buttermilk, room temperature
2 large eggs
1 large egg yolk

Vanilla ice cream
Spiced Syrup (see recipe)

Preheat oven to 350°F. Butter and flour 2 nonstick mini Bundt pans (6 cakes per pan). Sift dry ingredients into large bowl. Whisk 1¾ cups hot water and tea powder in another large bowl to blend. Whisk honey and next 4 ingredients into chai mixture to blend. Stir into flour mixture until blended. Divide batter among Bundt pans (about ½ cup per pan).

Bake cakes until toothpick inserted near centers comes out clean, about 25 minutes. Invert immediately onto rack. Cool 10 minutes. Serve warm with scoop of vanilla ice cream drizzled with Spiced Syrup. (*Cakes can be made 1 day ahead. Rewarm briefly in microwave.*)

Can be found in the coffee and tea section of most supermarkets.

MAKES 12

Spiced Syrup

2 cups (packed) golden brown sugar
2 cups water
¾ cup dark corn syrup
1½ tablespoons fresh lemon juice
1 teaspoon ground cinnamon
½ teaspoon vanilla extract

Stir all ingredients in heavy large deep saucepan over medium-low heat until sugar dissolves. Attach candy thermometer to side of pan (do not allow tip to touch bottom). Increase heat to high. Boil without stirring until thermometer registers 220°F, occasionally swirling pan and brushing down sides with wet pastry brush, about 12 minutes (time will vary depending on size of pan). Strain syrup into medium bowl. Cool to room temperature. (*Can be made 1 day ahead. Let stand at room temperature. Rewarm before serving.*)

MAKES ABOUT 2⅔ CUPS

Rich and Sticky Gingerbread with Marmalade

1²/₃ cups self-rising flour
1½ teaspoons ground ginger
½ cup (1 stick) unsalted butter, room temperature
¾ cup robust-flavored (dark) molasses
2 large eggs
1 cup orange marmalade
½ cup golden raisins
⅓ cup chopped crystallized ginger (about 2 ounces)

Preheat oven to 325°F. Butter and flour 9x9x2-inch metal baking pan; line bottom with parchment paper.

Sift flour and ground ginger into medium bowl. Using electric mixer, beat butter in large bowl until fluffy. Beat in molasses. Beat in flour mixture in 3 additions alternately with eggs, 1 at a time. Beat in marmalade, then raisins and crystallized ginger. Transfer to prepared baking pan.

Bake cake until tester inserted into center comes out clean, about 38 minutes. Cool cake completely in pan on rack. (*Can be made 1 day ahead. Cover and let stand at room temperature.*)

Cut cake into 9 squares. Cut each square in half, making eighteen 1½x3-inch pieces.

MAKES 18 PIECES

Dessert Buffet for 18

Champagne

Caramelized Pistachio, Walnut, and Almond Tart
(*page 185*)

Ginger-Lime Coconut Cake with Marshmallow Frosting
(*page 202*)

Rich and Sticky Gingerbread with Marmalade
(*at left, pictured at left*)

Dark Chocolate Oatmeal Cookies
(*double recipe; page 227*)

Cheesecake

Chocolate Truffles

Strawberries

Coffee and *Tea*

Individual Berry Trifles

½ cup plus 4 tablespoons (about) sugar

¼ cup all purpose flour

6 large egg yolks

2 cups half and half

1 vanilla bean, split lengthwise

1 cup coarsely crushed amaretti cookies (Italian macaroons; about 24)*

12 soft ladyfingers (sponge-cake variety), torn into small cubes

⅔ cup (about) Drambuie (Scotch-based liqueur) or Scotch

2 ½-pint containers fresh blackberries

2 ½-pint containers fresh raspberries

1 cup chilled whipping cream

¼ cup Scotch

Slivered almonds, toasted

Mix ½ cup sugar and flour in heavy large saucepan. Add yolks; whisk until smooth. Gradually whisk in half and half. Scrape in seeds from vanilla bean; add bean. Whisk constantly over medium-high heat until pastry cream thickens and boils, about 6 minutes. Press plastic wrap onto surface; chill at least 6 hours and up to 2 days.

Arrange eight 10- to 12-ounce wine goblets on work surface. Blend amaretti crumbs and ladyfinger pieces in small bowl. Spoon 1 tablespoon crumb mixture into each goblet. Sprinkle each with 1 generous teaspoon Drambuie. Top each with 2 generous tablespoons pastry cream, then 4 blackberries and 4 raspberries. Sprinkle berries with ¼ teaspoon sugar. Repeat layering 1 more time.

Beat whipping cream, ¼ cup Scotch, and 2 tablespoons sugar in medium bowl until cream holds peaks. Spoon large dollop of whipped cream onto each trifle; sprinkle with almonds. (*Can be made 1 day ahead. Cover and chill.*)

Available in some supermarkets and Italian markets.

MAKES 8

Vermont Maple Bread Pudding with Walnut Praline

PRALINE

Nonstick vegetable oil spray

2 cups sugar

1 cup walnuts, toasted, chopped

BREAD PUDDING

8 large eggs

1 quart whipping cream

1 cup sugar

1 cup maple syrup, plus more for drizzling

1 tablespoon vanilla extract

1 1-pound loaf brioche or egg bread, torn into bite-size pieces

Vanilla ice cream

FOR PRALINE: Spray rimmed baking sheet with nonstick spray. Stir sugar and ¼ cup water in heavy small saucepan over medium heat until sugar dissolves. Increase heat to high and boil without stirring until mixture turns deep amber color, occasionally swirling pan and brushing down sides with wet pastry brush, about 7 minutes. Stir in nuts. Quickly spread nuts on prepared sheet. Cool. Chop praline into small pieces. *(Can be made 1 day ahead. Store in airtight container at room temperature.)*

FOR BREAD PUDDING: Whisk eggs, cream, sugar, 1 cup maple syrup, and vanilla in large bowl to blend. Add brioche; stir to coat. Let stand at room temperature 1 hour, stirring occasionally.

Preheat oven to 375°F. Butter 13x9x2-inch baking dish. Transfer bread mixture to prepared dish. Bake until puffed and golden and toothpick inserted into center comes out clean, about 40 minutes. Cool slightly. Cut into 6 to 8 pieces. Place 1 piece pudding on each plate. Place scoop of ice cream atop pudding, drizzle with maple syrup, sprinkle with praline, and serve.

6 TO 8 SERVINGS

Classic Steak Dinner for 8

Skewered Rosemary Shrimp with Mint Pesto
(page 20)

Roast Beef Tenderloin with Merlot and Shallots
(page 49)

Mashed Potatoes

Creamed Spinach

Cabernet Sauvignon

Individual Berry Trifles
(opposite, pictured opposite)

Chocolate Panna Cotta with Port- and Balsamic-Glazed Cherries

PANNA COTTA

Canola oil

1 cup whole milk

2¼ teaspoons unflavored gelatin

2 cups whipping cream

½ cup sugar

5 ounces bittersweet or semisweet chocolate, chopped

½ teaspoon vanilla extract

CHERRIES

1 pound cherries, stemmed, pitted

¾ cup ruby Port

½ cup sugar

2 tablespoons balsamic vinegar

Port wine and balsamic vinegar deepen the fresh fruit flavors in the cherry sauce. Be sure to get started at least one day ahead; the panna cotta custards must chill for 24 hours before serving.

FOR PANNA COTTA: Brush six ¾-cup glass custard cups with canola oil. Pour milk into medium bowl. Sprinkle gelatin over; let stand until gelatin softens, about 5 minutes.

Stir cream and sugar in heavy medium saucepan over medium-high heat until sugar dissolves. Bring to boil; remove from heat. Add chocolate; whisk until melted. Whisk warm chocolate mixture into gelatin mixture; stir to dissolve. Stir in vanilla. Working in 2 batches, transfer mixture to blender and use only 3 on/off turns to just fully blend mixture (do not overmix). Divide mixture among custard cups. Cover and chill 24 hours. *(Can be made 2 days ahead. Keep chilled.)*

FOR CHERRIES: Stir cherries, Port, sugar, and vinegar in heavy large skillet over high heat until sugar dissolves. Bring to boil; reduce heat to medium and simmer until cherries are soft and wooden spoon leaves path in sauce when drawn across bottom of skillet, about 15 minutes. Remove from heat. Cool to room temperature. *(Can be made 2 days ahead. Cover and refrigerate. Bring to room temperature before continuing.)*

Set custard cups in large baking dish. Pour enough hot water into dish to come halfway up sides of cups. Let stand 1½ minutes. Take cups out of water; wipe bottoms dry. Invert each onto plate, shaking gently to dislodge panna cotta. Spoon cherries and sauce over panna cottas and serve.

MAKES 6

Warm Jasmine Rice Puddings with Passion Fruit

½ cup raisins
3 tablespoons Malibu rum or other coconut-flavored rum

1½ cups nonfat milk
1¼ cups canned unsweetened coconut milk*
¾ cup whole milk
1 cinnamon stick
½ teaspoon salt
½ vanilla bean, halved lengthwise

1¼ cups jasmine rice
6 tablespoons plus ¼ cup sugar

1 cup chilled whipping cream
2½ teaspoons grated lime peel

6 passion fruits, halved, juice and seeds scooped into bowl

Combine raisins and rum in bowl. Let stand at room temperature while preparing pudding.

Combine nonfat milk and next 4 ingredients in heavy medium saucepan. Scrape in seeds from vanilla bean; add bean. Bring to simmer; remove from heat. Allow to steep uncovered 1 hour. Strain coconut broth.

Rinse rice in medium bowl of cold water. Drain. Repeat 2 more times. Cook 1 cup coconut broth and rice in heavy medium saucepan over medium-high heat until almost all liquid is absorbed, stirring constantly, about 3 minutes. Add remaining coconut broth; cook over low heat until rice is tender, stirring frequently, about 13 minutes. Remove from heat. Stir in 6 tablespoons sugar (mixture will be thick). Transfer to large bowl; cool.

Whip cream in medium bowl until cream holds peaks. Fold half of whipped cream into cooled rice. Drain raisins. Stir raisins and lime peel into rice. Fold in remaining whipped cream. Divide mixture among eight ¾-cup ramekins or custard cups.

Preheat broiler. Sprinkle ½ tablespoon sugar over each pudding. Place puddings on rimmed baking sheet. Broil until sugar caramelizes, watching closely to prevent burning, about 3 minutes. Spoon passion fruit over puddings.

Available at many supermarkets and at Indian, Southeast Asian, and Latin American markets.

MAKES 8

Double-Chocolate Soufflés

2 tablespoons (¼ stick) unsalted butter

2 tablespoons all purpose flour

1 cup whole milk

8 ounces bittersweet or semisweet chocolate, chopped

6 tablespoons sugar, divided

1 ounce unsweetened chocolate, chopped

4 large eggs, separated

¼ teaspoon salt

Lightly sweetened whipped cream

This luscious dessert has some helpful do-ahead hints. The soufflés can be made a week ahead and frozen, or two days ahead and refrigerated.

Butter eight ¾-cup ramekins or custard cups; dust with sugar. Arrange dishes on rimmed baking sheet.

Melt 2 tablespoons butter in heavy medium saucepan over medium heat. Add 2 tablespoons flour; whisk until mixture is bubbling, about 1 minute. Increase heat to medium-high. Gradually whisk in 1 cup milk. Cook until mixture thickens and boils, whisking constantly, about 2 minutes. Remove from heat. Add bittersweet chocolate, 4 tablespoons sugar, and unsweetened chocolate; whisk until melted and smooth. Pour soufflé base into large bowl. Cool to room temperature, stirring occasionally.

Whisk egg yolks into soufflé base. Using electric mixer, beat egg whites and salt in medium bowl until soft peaks form. Gradually add remaining 2 tablespoons sugar, beating until stiff and glossy. Fold ¼ of whites into soufflé base. Fold in remaining whites in 2 additions. Divide soufflé mixture among prepared ramekins. (Can be prepared ahead. Cover and refrigerate up to 2 days or freeze up to 1 week; do not thaw frozen soufflés before baking.)

Preheat oven to 400°F. Bake soufflés uncovered on rimmed baking sheet until puffed and centers move slightly when sheet is shaken gently, about 17 minutes for fresh or chilled soufflés or 22 minutes for frozen.

Serve chocolate soufflés immediately with sweetened whipped cream.

8 SERVINGS

Ice Cream Truffles

½ pint (about) vanilla ice cream
½ pint (about) coffee ice cream
½ pint (about) chocolate ice cream

20 ounces bittersweet (not unsweetened) or semisweet chocolate, chopped
1½ tablespoons vegetable oil

2 cups sliced almonds, toasted
2 cups sweetened flaked coconut (about 5 ounces), lightly toasted
1½ cups shelled natural pistachios, chopped

Line large rimmed baking sheet with waxed paper. Using 1½-inch round ice cream scoop or round 1 tablespoon measuring spoon and working quickly, scoop out 8 round balls each of vanilla, coffee, and chocolate ice cream, placing ice cream on prepared baking sheet. Freeze ice cream at least 8 hours (ice cream must be very firm).

Combine chopped chocolate and vegetable oil in large metal bowl. Place bowl over saucepan of barely simmering water; stir until chocolate is melted and smooth. Remove bowl from over water. Cool chocolate until just barely lukewarm.

Place almonds, coconut, and pistachios in 3 separate medium bowls. Line 3 pie dishes or plates with waxed paper. Working with 1 vanilla ice cream ball at a time and working quickly, drop into lukewarm melted chocolate. Using fork, turn to coat and lift out chocolate-coated ball. Drop ball off fork into bowl with almonds, using hands to turn to coat. Place truffle in 1 prepared pie dish. Repeat with remaining vanilla ice cream balls, melted chocolate, and almonds; place in freezer. Repeat same procedure, dropping coffee ice cream balls into melted chocolate, then coconut, and dropping chocolate ice cream balls into melted chocolate, then pistachios. Freeze all ice cream truffles until firm, about 2 hours, then cover and keep frozen. (*Can be made 3 days ahead. Keep frozen.*)

Place 1 almond-coated ice cream truffle, 1 coconut-coated truffle, and 1 pistachio-coated truffle on each of 8 plates and serve.

MAKES 24

Frozen Tropical Terrine with Mango-Blackberry Sauce

1 7-ounce package sweetened flaked coconut, toasted, divided
2 pints pineapple-coconut ice cream, divided
1 pint mango sorbet
1 pint boysenberry sorbet

1 large mango, peeled, pitted, sliced
2 ½-pint containers blackberries
¼ cup sugar
1 vanilla bean, split lengthwise

Line 9x5x2¾-inch metal loaf pan with 2 layers of plastic wrap in each direction, leaving overhang. Sprinkle 1¼ cups toasted coconut over bottom of pan. Microwave 1 pint pineapple-coconut ice cream on low in two or three 10-second intervals until slightly softened. Drop ice cream by large spoonfuls over coconut in pan, then spread in even layer; freeze 15 minutes. Microwave mango sorbet on low in two or three 10-second intervals until slightly softened. Drop sorbet by large spoonfuls atop ice cream, then spread in even layer; freeze 15 minutes. Repeat with boysenberry sorbet, then remaining 1 pint ice cream. Sprinkle remaining coconut over top; press to adhere (filling will extend slightly above pan). Cover with plastic wrap overhang; freeze overnight. (*Can be made 3 days ahead. Keep frozen.*)

Combine mango, blackberries, and sugar in medium bowl. Scrape in seeds from vanilla bean; add bean and toss. Let stand at room temperature until juices form, tossing occasionally, about 2 hours. (*Can be made 4 hours ahead. Cover and chill.*) Discard vanilla bean.

Using plastic wrap as aid, lift terrine out of pan; remove plastic wrap. Cut terrine into ¾-inch-thick slices. Place on plates; spoon sauce over and serve.

8 SERVINGS

Purchased pineapple-coconut ice cream and mango and boysenberry sorbets make this dessert easy. The terrine needs to freeze overnight before serving.

Pink Grapefruit, Strawberry, and Champagne Granita with Sugared Strawberries

1¼ cups sugar, divided
¾ cup water
1 cup small strawberries, hulled (about 6 ounces)
¾ cup fresh pink or ruby grapefruit juice
2¼ cups chilled brut Champagne

1½ teaspoons grated lemon peel
9 teaspoons mascarpone cheese*
18 whole small strawberries

Use a Microplane grater or the smallest holes on a box grater to remove the lemon peel in thin, fine pieces. Any delicate buttery cookies—such as pirouettes, small shortbreads, or tender madeleines—would be delicious with the granita.

Stir ¾ cup sugar and ¾ cup water in large saucepan over low heat until sugar dissolves. Cool. Puree 1 cup strawberries in processor. Whisk ½ cup puree into sugar syrup. Mix in grapefruit juice, then Champagne. Pour mixture into 8-inch square metal baking pan. Freeze mixture until firm, stirring every 2 hours, about 6 hours. (*Can be made 2 days ahead. Cover; keep frozen.*)

Mix remaining ½ cup sugar and lemon peel in pie plate. Spread ½ teaspoon mascarpone around pointed tip half of each whole strawberry. Dip in lemon sugar to coat mascarpone.

Moisten rims of 6 Martini glasses with water; dip rims into remaining lemon sugar. Scrape fork across surface of granita to form ice shavings. Mound granita in glasses. Garnish with sugared berries and serve.

Italian cream cheese, available in some supermarkets and at Italian markets.

6 SERVINGS

Lemon-Raspberry Ice Cream Bombes

½ cup sugar

¼ cup fresh lemon juice

2 large egg yolks

1½ teaspoons (packed) finely grated lemon peel

⅛ teaspoon salt

½ cup chilled whipping cream

1 quart vanilla ice cream

¾ cup raspberry sorbet

2 cups fresh raspberries
Fresh mint sprigs (optional)
Lemon peel

Whisk sugar, lemon juice, yolks, peel, and salt to blend in top of double boiler. Place over simmering water (do not allow bottom of pan to touch water). Whisk until mixture thickens and thermometer inserted into mixture registers 160°F, about 6 minutes. Transfer mixture to medium bowl. Chill until cold, about 45 minutes.

Beat cream in another medium bowl until cream holds peaks. Fold into lemon mixture in 3 additions. Cover and chill at least 6 hours and up to 1 day.

Line six ¾-cup custard cups with foil, leaving generous overhang. Slightly soften quart of ice cream in microwave at low setting in 10-second intervals. Measure ½ cup ice cream and place in 1 prepared custard cup. Using back of teaspoon and dipping spoon in glass of warm water as needed, press ice cream in even layer over bottom and up sides of cup, creating hollow in center. Place cup in freezer. Repeat with remaining 5 prepared cups. Return remaining ice cream in quart to freezer. Freeze ice cream in cups 1 hour.

Spoon 2 tablespoons sorbet into hollow in center of each cup and pack firmly. Return cups to freezer for 1 hour.

Divide lemon cream among cups, smoothing tops. Freeze 1 hour.

Resoften remaining ice cream in quart container in microwave at low setting in 10-second intervals. Spread 2 tablespoons ice cream over lemon cream in each cup, covering completely. Fold foil overhang over bombes to cover; freeze at least 3 hours and up to 2 days.

Open foil on bombes; turn bombes out onto dishes. Peel off foil. Spoon fresh berries alongside. Garnish with mint sprigs, if desired, and lemon peel.

MAKES 6

Caramel and Crème Fraîche Sundaes with Cashews

ICE CREAM

   2 cups whole milk, divided

   8 large egg yolks

   1 cup whipping cream

  ¾ cup (packed) dark brown sugar

  ⅛ teaspoon salt

7½ to 8 ounces crème fraîche or sour cream

   1 teaspoon vanilla extract

CRÈME FRAÎCHE CARAMEL SAUCE

1½ cups sugar

   1 large vanilla bean, split lengthwise

  ⅓ cup whipping cream

  ⅓ cup crème fraîche or sour cream

   3 tablespoons unsalted butter

CASHEWS

   1 cup raw whole cashews

2½ tablespoons vegetable oil

   4 teaspoons coarse kosher salt

      Whipped cream

FOR ICE CREAM: Whisk ½ cup milk and egg yolks in medium bowl. Bring 1½ cups milk, cream, sugar, and salt to simmer in heavy large saucepan over medium-high heat, whisking until sugar dissolves. Gradually whisk hot milk mixture into yolk mixture; return to same saucepan. Stir over medium heat until custard thickens enough to leave path on back of spoon when finger is drawn across, about 6 minutes (do not boil). Strain custard into medium bowl. Place over large bowl of ice water and cool, stirring often. Whisk in crème fraîche and vanilla. Process in ice cream maker according to manufacturer's instructions. Transfer to container. Cover and freeze at least 6 hours and up to 3 days.

FOR CRÈME FRAÎCHE CARAMEL SAUCE: Stir sugar and ½ cup water in heavy medium saucepan over low heat until sugar dissolves, occasionally brushing down sides of pan with wet pastry brush. Scrape in seeds from vanilla bean; add bean. Increase heat and boil without stirring until syrup is deep amber color, occasionally brushing down sides and swirling pan, about 16 minutes (time will vary depending on size of pan). Remove pan from heat. Mix in cream, crème fraîche, and butter (mixture will bubble vigorously). Stir until smooth. Discard vanilla bean. *(Can be made 3 days ahead. Cover and chill. Rewarm slightly before serving.)*

FOR CASHEWS: Preheat oven to 350°F. Mix nuts, oil, and salt in bowl. Spread on baking sheet. Bake until nuts are golden, stirring often, about 12 minutes. Cool. *(Can be made 1 day ahead. Store airtight.)*

Scoop ice cream into dishes. Spoon warm caramel sauce over. Top sundaes with whipped cream and cashews.

MAKES 6 TO 8

Chocolate-Orange Sorbet

    4 cups water
    ⅔ cup sugar
    1 tablespoon instant coffee crystals
    ½ cup frozen orange juice concentrate, thawed
    1 pound bittersweet or semisweet chocolate, chopped

Bring first 3 ingredients to boil in large saucepan over medium-high heat, stirring until sugar dissolves. Mix in orange juice concentrate. Reduce heat to low. Add chocolate and whisk until smooth. Chill uncovered 4 hours, stirring occasionally.

Process sorbet mixture in ice cream maker according to manufacturer's instructions. Transfer to container. Cover; freeze at least 6 hours and up to 3 days.

MAKES ABOUT 7 CUPS

Housewarming Party for 8

Chili with Sausage and Jalapeño
(page 54)

Skillet Cornbread with Roasted Poblano and Oregano
(page 167)

Beer

Caramel and Crème Fraîche Sundaes with Cashews
(opposite, pictured opposite)

Strawberry and Prosecco Fizz with Lemon Sorbet

 3 pints strawberries, divided
 1/3 cup plus 1/4 cup sugar

 3 pints lemon sorbet
 1 750-ml bottle chilled Prosecco or brut Champagne

Hull 1 1/2 pints strawberries; cut in half. Puree berries and 1/3 cup sugar in processor until very smooth. Transfer to small bowl and chill well, at least 1 hour and up to 2 hours.

Place half of berry puree and half of lemon sorbet in processor. Slowly add 3/4 cup Prosecco; blend until mixture is thick and slushy. Transfer to medium bowl. Repeat with remaining berry mixture, sorbet, and Prosecco. Freeze at least 2 hours. Place Champagne stopper on remaining Prosecco and refrigerate. (*Sorbet mixture can be made 1 day ahead. Keep frozen.*)

Hull remaining 1 1/2 pints berries; quarter lengthwise. Mix berries with 1/4 cup sugar in large bowl; chill 1 to 2 hours.

Spoon sorbet mixture into 8 parfait glasses. Top with remaining Prosecco and sugared strawberries.

8 SERVINGS

Peppermint Ice Cream with Hot Fudge Sauce

SAUCE
 2 cups powdered sugar
 12 ounces semisweet chocolate chips (about 2 cups)
 1 12-ounce can evaporated milk
 1/2 cup (1 stick) unsalted butter
 2 ounces unsweetened chocolate, chopped
 1 teaspoon vanilla extract

ICE CREAM
 2 1/2-gallon cartons vanilla ice cream, softened slightly
 4 7.5-ounce bags red-and-white-striped hard peppermint candies, coarsely crushed

FOR SAUCE: Stir all ingredients in heavy large saucepan over medium heat until chocolates and butter melt and sauce is smooth. (*Can be prepared 1 week ahead. Cover and refrigerate. Rewarm before using.*)

FOR ICE CREAM: Place ice cream in large bowl; mix in peppermint candies. Cover and freeze at least 6 hours. (*Can be made 2 days ahead. Keep frozen.*)

Scoop ice cream into bowls. Pour warm fudge sauce over.

14 SERVINGS

Frozen Pumpkin Mousse with Walnut-Toffee Crunch

CRUNCH

Vegetable oil

1 cup walnut pieces (about 4 ounces)

2/3 cup toffee bits (such as Skor; about 3½ ounces)

4 teaspoons (packed) dark brown sugar

⅛ teaspoon salt

1 tablespoon unsalted butter, melted

MOUSSE

2 cups chilled heavy whipping cream, divided

¾ cup sugar

5 large egg yolks

1¼ cups canned pure pumpkin

2 tablespoons dark rum

1¼ teaspoons vanilla extract

¾ teaspoon ground cinnamon

½ teaspoon ground ginger

¼ teaspoon ground nutmeg

¼ teaspoon salt

⅛ teaspoon ground allspice

4 cinnamon sticks

FOR CRUNCH: Preheat oven to 350°F. Line rimmed baking sheet with foil; brush generously with oil. Toss nuts, toffee bits, sugar, and salt in medium bowl to blend. Add butter; toss to coat. Place in center of prepared sheet; pat to single layer. Bake until toffee bits are soft (but retain shape), about 15 minutes. Cool. Transfer to work surface; chop coarsely.

FOR MOUSSE: Whisk ¾ cup cream, sugar, and yolks in heavy medium saucepan to blend. Stir over medium-low heat until thickened to pudding consistency, about 10 minutes (do not boil). Transfer to large bowl. Mix in pumpkin and next 7 ingredients. Refrigerate uncovered until cold, stirring occasionally, about 40 minutes.

Beat 1¼ cups cream in another large bowl until cream holds peaks. Transfer ½ cup whipped cream to medium bowl for garnish; cover and chill. Fold remaining whipped cream into pumpkin mixture. Cover; chill mousse at least 4 hours and up to 1 day.

In each of 4 medium (10-ounce) goblets, layer ⅓ cup mousse and generous tablespoon crunch. Repeat 2 more times (some crunch may be left). If necessary, whisk reserved ½ cup whipped cream to soft peaks. Pipe or drop dollop of cream onto mousse in each goblet. Cover; freeze overnight. (*Can be made 2 days ahead. Keep frozen. Let stand at room temperature 30 minutes before serving.*) Garnish with cinnamon sticks.

4 SERVINGS

Classic Date Bars

1½ cups water
1½ cups chopped pitted dates
  1 teaspoon vanilla extract

1½ cups all purpose flour
  1 cup (packed) dark brown sugar
  1 cup old-fashioned oats
1½ teaspoons ground cinnamon
  ½ teaspoon baking soda
  ½ teaspoon salt
  ¾ cup (1½ sticks) unsalted butter, diced, room temperature

Preheat oven to 350°F. Butter 8x8-inch metal baking pan. Bring 1½ cups water to simmer in medium saucepan. Add dates; simmer until very soft and thick, stirring occasionally, about 10 minutes. Cool to room temperature. Stir in vanilla.

Combine flour, sugar, oats, cinnamon, baking soda, and salt in large bowl; stir to blend. Add butter. Using fingertips, rub in until moist clumps form. Press half of oat mixture evenly over bottom of prepared pan. Spread date mixture over. Sprinkle with remaining oat mixture; press gently to adhere. Bake until brown at edges and golden brown and set in center, about 40 minutes. Cool completely in pan on rack. Cut into bars and serve.

MAKES 16

Dark Chocolate Oatmeal Cookies

¾ cup all purpose flour

¼ cup unsweetened cocoa powder

½ teaspoon baking soda

¼ teaspoon salt

½ cup (1 stick) unsalted butter, room temperature

½ cup sugar

½ teaspoon vanilla extract

2 tablespoons steel-cut oats

¼ cup semisweet chocolate chips

These rich treats get their chewy-crunchy texture from Scottish pinhead (steel-cut) oats. For a more tender cookie, use old-fashioned oats.

Preheat oven to 350°F. Butter large rimmed baking sheet. Sift first 4 ingredients into medium bowl. Using electric mixer, beat butter in large bowl until fluffy. Add sugar and vanilla; beat until blended. Add flour mixture and beat until moist clumps form. Mix in oats with spatula until evenly distributed (dough will be very firm). Add chocolate chips and knead gently to blend.

Using moistened palms, shape 1 generous tablespoon dough into ball. Place on prepared sheet; flatten to 2-inch round. Repeat with remaining dough, spacing rounds about 2 inches apart.

Bake cookies until centers are slightly firm and tops are cracked, about 14 minutes. Cool on sheet.

MAKES 12

Chocolate Brownies
with Peanut Butter Frosting

BROWNIES

  Nonstick vegetable oil spray
5 ounces unsweetened chocolate, coarsely chopped
4 ounces bittersweet (not unsweetened) or semisweet chocolate, coarsely chopped
½ cup (1 stick) unsalted butter
1½ cups sugar
4 large eggs
1 teaspoon vanilla extract
½ cup all purpose flour
¼ teaspoon salt

FROSTING

1 cup creamy peanut butter (do not use old-fashioned or freshly ground)
3 tablespoons unsalted butter, room temperature
⅔ cup powdered sugar
1 teaspoon vanilla extract

FOR BROWNIES: Preheat oven to 350°F. Line 13x9x2-inch baking pan with foil, leaving 2-inch overhang on both short sides. Spray foil with nonstick spray. Combine both chocolates and butter in heavy small saucepan. Stir over low heat until melted and smooth. Cool to barely lukewarm. Using electric mixer, beat sugar, eggs, and vanilla extract in large bowl on high speed until mixture thickens and is pale yellow, about 5 minutes. Reduce mixer speed to low; beat in flour and salt, then melted chocolate mixture. Transfer to prepared baking pan.

Bake brownies until tester inserted into center comes out with moist crumbs still attached, about 20 minutes. Transfer baking pan to rack; cool 15 minutes. Press gently on edges of brownies to level with center. Cool completely in baking pan.

FOR FROSTING: Combine peanut butter and butter in medium bowl. Using electric mixer, beat until smooth. Add powdered sugar and vanilla extract and beat until well blended and smooth. Spread frosting evenly over brownies in pan. Refrigerate at least 1 hour. Using foil as aid, lift out brownies from pan. Cut into squares. (*Can be prepared 1 day ahead. Cover and keep refrigerated. Let stand at room temperature 30 minutes before serving.*)

MAKES 24

Open-House Buffet
for 16

Fresh Crab Dip
(page 16)

Sweet and Spicy Herbed Hazelnuts
(page 16)

Crudités with Hummus

Purchased Baked Ham

Coriander Rice
(page 146)

Carrot Salad with Orange, Green Olives, and Green Onions
(page 158)

Chive Popovers
(page 166)

Sauvignon Blanc **and** *Merlot*

Sparkling Water

Chocolate Brownies with Peanut Butter Frosting
(at left, pictured opposite)

Lemon-Coconut Bars
(page 232)

Coffee **and** *Tea*

Fruit and Nut Cereal Cookies

        2   cups old-fashioned oats
      1¼   cups whole wheat flour
        1   cup all purpose flour
        1   cup Grape-Nuts cereal
        ½   cup wheat germ*
        ½   cup oat bran*
        2   teaspoons baking soda
        2   cups (4 sticks) unsalted butter, room temperature
        2   large eggs
        1   cup (packed) golden brown sugar
        ½   cup sugar
        1   tablespoon vanilla extract
        1   cup almonds (about 5 ounces), toasted, coarsely chopped
        1   cup raisins (about 5 ounces)
        1   cup chopped pitted dates (about 8 ounces)

      14   whole pitted dates, split lengthwise in half

Preheat oven to 350°F. Mix oats, both flours, Grape-Nuts, wheat germ, oat bran, and baking soda in large bowl to blend. Using electric mixer, beat butter in another large bowl until creamy. Add eggs, both sugars, and vanilla; beat until smooth. Add cereal mixture; stir just until blended. Mix in almonds, raisins, and 1 cup chopped dates. (*Can be prepared 1 week ahead. Cover and chill. Let soften at room temperature before continuing.*)

Line 2 heavy large baking sheets with parchment paper. Using 2-ounce ice cream scoop or ¼-cup measure as aid, scoop dough onto prepared baking sheets, spacing mounds 2 inches apart. Using damp fingers, press cookies to ½-inch-thick rounds. Press 1 date half into center of each cookie.

Bake cookies 1 sheet at a time until brown on top, about 15 minutes. Let cookies stand on baking sheet 10 minutes before transferring to rack to cool. (*Can be made 8 hours ahead. Let stand at room temperature.*) Serve slightly warm or at room temperature.

Sold in the health foods section or cereal section of some supermarkets and at natural foods stores.

MAKES 28

Pistachio and Vanilla Shortbread

1½ cups all purpose flour
½ cup sugar
½ cup semolina flour*
1 cup (2 sticks) chilled unsalted butter, cut into ½-inch cubes
1½ teaspoons grated lemon peel
1 teaspoon vanilla extract
1 cup shelled natural pistachios (about 4 ounces), coarsely chopped

Traditional shortbread is baked in molds. In this modern version, the dough is simply pressed into a pan, baked, and cut into squares. Grated lemon peel cuts the buttery richness, and semolina flour adds texture.

Preheat oven to 325°F. Butter 13x9x2-inch metal baking pan. Combine all purpose flour, sugar, and semolina flour in processor; blend 5 seconds. Add butter, lemon peel, and vanilla. Using on/off turns, blend until coarse meal forms. Turn dough out into bowl. Add nuts and knead gently to combine. Press dough evenly over bottom of prepared pan. Using fork, pierce dough all over.

Bake shortbread until pale brown in center and golden at edges, about 35 minutes. Cool in pan on rack 10 minutes. Cut lengthwise into 4 strips, then cut each strip crosswise into 6 squares. Cool completely in pan. *(Can be made 1 day ahead. Cover tightly with foil; store at room temperature.)*

Semolina flour, often labeled "pasta flour," is sold in some supermarkets and at specialty foods stores and Italian markets.

MAKES 24 COOKIES

Lemon-Coconut Bars

CRUST

    1 cup all purpose flour

  ¼ cup sugar

  ¼ teaspoon salt

  ¾ cup sweetened flaked coconut, toasted, cooled

    6 tablespoons (¾ stick) chilled unsalted butter, cut into ½-inch cubes

FILLING

  ¾ cup sugar

    2 large eggs

  ¼ cup fresh lemon juice

    1 tablespoon (packed) finely grated lemon peel

    1 teaspoon all purpose flour

  ½ teaspoon baking powder

      Pinch of salt

  ¼ cup powdered sugar

FOR CRUST: Preheat oven to 350°F. Line 8x8x2-inch metal baking pan with foil, leaving overhang. Butter foil. Combine flour, sugar, and salt in processor; blend 5 seconds. Add coconut and butter; process until mixture resembles fine meal and begins to clump together. Gather dough into ball. Press dough evenly over bottom of prepared pan. Bake crust until golden at edges, about 25 minutes.

MEANWHILE, PREPARE FILLING: Combine ¾ cup sugar, eggs, lemon juice, lemon peel, flour, baking powder, and salt in processor. Blend filling until smooth.

Remove crust from oven. Pour filling evenly over hot crust. Return to oven and bake until filling begins to brown at edges and is just set and springy to touch in center, about 30 minutes. Transfer pan to rack; cool lemon bars completely.

Using foil as aid, transfer lemon bars to work surface. Flatten foil edges. Cut into 16 bars. Sift powdered sugar over. (*Can be prepared 5 days ahead. Store bar cookies airtight in single layer in refrigerator.*)

MAKES 16

Index

Page numbers in *italics* indicate color photographs.

Acknowledgments

RECIPES

A.O.C., Los Angeles, California
Abacrombie Fine Food &
Accommodations, Baltimore,
Maryland
Adega Restaurant + Wine Bar,
Denver, Colorado
Bruce Aidells
Elvena and Eduardo Alvariño
José Andrés, Jaleo, Washington, DC
Melanie Barnard
Monica Bhide
Lena Cederham Birnbaum
Kimberly Boyce
Wayne Harley Brachman
Bette and Jeffrey Butler
Café Soriah, Eugene, Oregon
Ceiba, Washington, DC
Charlotte Street Grill and Pub,
Asheville, North Carolina
Colin Cowie
Lane Crowther
Cucina Biazzi, Ashland, Oregon
Delfina, San Francisco, California
Lori De Mori
Dinosaur Bar-B-Que, Rochester,
New York
Brooke Dojny
Elements Café, Haddon Heights,
New Jersey
Elizabeth Falkner
The Farm Café, Portland, Oregon

FireLake Grill House & Cocktail
Bar, Minneapolis, Minnesota
Flatiron Lounge, New York
Bobby Flay
Claudia Fleming
Robyn Fuoco, Mainly Café and
Bakery, Philadelphia, Pennsylvania
Glory: An American Bistro,
Chicago, Illinois
Suzanne Goin
Rozanne Gold
Dorie Greenspan
Gerry Hayden, Amuse,
New York, New York
Sabrina Henderson
Florencia Attademo-Hirt and Brian Hirt
Huckleberry's Fresh Market,
Spokane, Washington
Jill Hough
Isa, San Francisco, California
Diane Ives
Cheryl and Bill Jamison
Zov Karamardian
Jeanne Thiel Kelley
George Kelso
Kristine Kidd
La Spiga, New Orleans, Louisiana
Sue Lawrence
David Lebovitz
Le Cirque 2000, New York, New York
Michelle and Daniel Lehmann
Rosemary Leicht
Hannah Levitz

Lady Claire Macdonald
Meriel Macdonald
Leslie Mackie
Donata Maggipinto
Martine, Salt Lake City, Utah
Janet Taylor McCracken
Ann Ferrell Millham and
Steve Millham
Monarch, St. Louis, Missouri
Selma Brown Morrow
Mother's Bistro & Bar,
Portland, Oregon
One Midtown Kitchen,
Atlanta, Georgia
Phat Thai, Aspen, Colorado
Anna Pump, Loaves & Fishes,
Sagaponack, New York
Jamie Purviance
Steven Raichlen
Victoria Abbott Riccardi
Susan Richardson
Rick Rodgers
Betty Rosbottom
Rouge, Houston, Texas
Cathy and George Sakellaris
Sarah Patterson Scott
Michael Shrader, Nine Restaurant
Group, Palm Springs, California
Martha Rose Shulman
Marie Simmons
Susan Simon
Simon Kitchen and Bar,
Las Vegas, Nevada

Spice Market, New York, New York
Tartine, San Francisco, California
Mark Taylor
Sarah Tenaglia
Annie and Joe Thomson
Tutti's, Ventura, California
Union Bar and Grille, Boston,
Massachusetts
Dede Wilson
Woodfire Grill, Atlanta, Georgia
Helen Yard

PHOTOGRAPHY

Noel Barnhurst
Wyatt Counts
Michael Falconer
Fran Gealer
Leo Gong
Lisa Hubbard
Brian Leatart
Ericka McConnell
Susan Gentry McWhinney
Pornchai Mittongtare
Gary Moss
Raymond Patrick
Scott Peterson
France Ruffenach
Charles Schiller
Mark Thomas
Julie Toy
Luca Trovato